It's Christmas!

Forty-eight Stories
and Three One-act Plays

Jan Bono

SANDRIDGE PUBLICATIONS

JAN BONO

First Printing, Fall 2011

Printed in the United States of America
Gorham Printing, Centralia, WA 98531

ISBN: 978-0-9838066-1-5

Contents

Introduction

I love Christmas!

The last Thanksgiving turkey sandwich is still in my hand when I fly into action, happily decorating every room of my home—and I do mean *every!*

Forty-six pictures on various walls are transformed into gaily-wrapped "presents," complete with ribbons and bows. No more than three presents have the same wrapping paper, and no two in a row have the same basic color scheme or bow pattern.

Most windows are outlined with colored lights; all receive snowflake treatments, some sparkly, some textured. Everyday beige and brown throw pillows are exchanged for dozens with bright red and green holiday designs. Ordinary oven mitts and kitchen towels are replaced with those displaying Santa's likeness.

Garlands hang everywhere: Across every arch, doorway, mirror, hutch, bookcase and fireplace span. Some garlands are gold, some are silver, but many are multi-colored red and green or red and silver, and I love the way they reflect the colored lights.

I put up four Christmas trees every year. Each one has its own unique set of decorations. The largest tree is 12 feet high. This behemoth in the living room takes an average of 10 strings of traditional twinkling lights and 160 brightly-colored ornaments. And tinsel. It *has* to have tinsel!

The bathroom shower curtain sports poinsettias, the towels and washcloths have holiday patterns and the toilet seat is covered with a yarn design of Santa's smiling face. Even the toilet paper has a crocheted cover resembling a holiday bell.

All this decorating is in preparation for my annual "knock your socks off" blow-out Christmas party. And the party is just one of the dozens of holiday activities I look forward to each year.

As I said before, *I love Christmas!*

And this holiday collection reflects that love. These selections are gleaned from my own family stories, former newspaper column, blog entries, personal observations, a little romantic seasonal fiction, the world's best Christmas poem (*according to my mother*) and the scripts of three of my holiday one-act plays.

Is the collection a bit eclectic? *Absolutely!* So there's sure to be plenty for everyone's enjoyment.

Dedicated
to those who keep Christmas
forever in their hearts

What's your Holiday I.Q.?

How do you handle the holidays? Are you a staunch holiday traditionalist, a free-thinking flexible rogue, or somewhere in between?

This 18-question quiz will help you identify your holiday style. And once you recognize and accept your personal style, you can use these results to justify telling your family to buzz off while you test the Christmas fudge for "Quality Control."

No cheating now! Mark your first initial primary gut-level immediate response to each question...*IN INK!*

ST. NICHOLAS AND COMPANY

Santa is
  s) a right jolly old elf
  h) the new year's Jenny Craig poster boy
  g) the first name of Barbara, Cruz, and Anita

Reindeer are
  s) delightful four-legged flying animals who pull Santa's sleigh
  h) members of a rock group called "The North Pole Nine"
  g) best served with gravy

Rudolph had

s) a nose so bright
h) a bunch of fair-weather friends
g) a terrible chronic sinus infection

HOLIDAY PREPARATIONS

Christmas wrap and ribbon
　　s) should be color complementary
　　h) is unnecessary if you have a large, plain, brown
　　　　paper bag
　　g) need not take up store display space until late
　　　　December 24

On your fireplace hearth you hang
　　s) the hundreds of cards you receive each year
　　h) a bright red fuzzy stocking with your name
　　　　embroidered on it
　　g) a pair of "Just My Size" pantyhose

Christmas cards are
　　s) carefully selected and signed with a personal
　　　　note
　　h) a complete waste of time, since nobody reads
　　　　them anyway
　　g) a communist plot by the USPS to boost year-end
　　　　stamp revenue

GIFT GIVING

The most romantic and desirable Christmas gift from
your true love is
　　s) lovingly handmade

h) Five Golden Rings
g) mutual funds

Mr. and Mrs. Claus' permanent mailing address is
s) at the North Pole
h) in the Bahamas
g) unlisted

It is more blessed to
s) give than to receive
h) return every unrequested gift for cash
g) become an atheist to avoid the whole Christmas madness

CHRISTMAS CAROLS

Dashing through the snow
s) is the first line of "Jingle Bells"
h) is a major cause of winter accidents
g) would be better punctuated with hyphens

Adeste Fideles is
s) "O Come All Ye Faithful" in Latin
h) the marriage vow of monogamy
g) the leader of Cuba

We three kings of Orient are
s) bearing gifts we traverse far
h) tried to smoke a rubber cigar
g) traveling now by black armored car

RELIGIOUS SIGNIFICANCE

Bethlehem
>   s) was the town where Jesus was born
>   h) changed her name to Elizabeth in the sixteenth century
>   g) is something a person with a cold coughs up

Jesus is
>   s) the reason for the season
>   h) a Spanish name pronounced "Hay-soose"
>   g) a mild oath used while assembling a bicycle

A manger is
>   s) a stable hay crib
>   h) the guy who's getting paid to coach the Mariners
>   g) a stray dog with large blotchy patches of fur missing

TRADITIONS

Mistletoe is
>   s) a good thing to stand under to catch a quick kiss
>   h) a good thing to stand under to catch a quick cold germ
>   g) what astronauts get instead of athlete's foot

Putting up a Christmas tree
>   s) brings the family closer during the holiday season
>   h) is a waste of good firewood
>   g) is the number one cause of divorce in America

The true Holiday Spirits are
- s) Christmas Past, Present, and Future
- h) Curly, Larry and Moe
- g) Rum and Eggnog

SCORING:

If you chose "S" as your answer to the majority of these questions, you are a virtual paragon of the Christmas Spirit, a real Saint, and I'll see you in church!

If "H" was your most chosen response, you're a Humbug, all right, but you're still redeemable.

A predominance of "G" answers indicate a certifiable Grinch. In order to survive this holiday season, I suggest immediately refilling your Prozac prescription.

In the event you honestly completed the entire quiz and no letter was chosen a significant number of times over than any other, Congratulations! You are one of the confused majority; your holiday season will be joyously stressful and you will handle each crisis with a healthy sense of humor.

Name that deer!

Although I was an elementary teacher the majority of my career, I never had children of my own. I often joked that I got my "kid fix" at work, but I was happy to occasionally cover for my friends who needed a babysitter on short notice.

Babysitting three-and-a-half-year-old Kendra was a true joy. She was an only child, the apple of her mother's eye, and quite articulate for her age. I must admit, I spoiled her rotten, taking her presents and playing games with her long past her usual bedtime. I don't know which one of us ended up having the most fun, as we always had such a great time.

One Saturday in early December, her mother called and asked me to come over "for a play date with Kendra" while she did her Christmas shopping "unassisted." I was only too happy to comply. "But you don't need to bring her any more toys," she said. "She's already got too many toys, and Christmas is just a couple weeks away."

Kendra met me at the door. "Aunt Jannie!" she exclaimed, hopping up and down excitedly. She stopped hopping and gave me a big hug. "What did you bring me?" she asked, in typical not-quite-four-year-old fashion.

"Kendra!" admonished her mother, "that's not polite!" She turned to me and smiled. "So what *did* you bring her?"

I sheepishly removed a new coloring book about animals from my tote bag. "I promise, it's educational!"

So before allowing a single mark in the book, I read the entire text to my young friend, pausing to comment and ask questions about the animals on each page.

Beneath the picture of several deer were the words, "Here are the deer. The largest deer is the American Moose." I asked her if she'd ever seen a live moose.

"I've seen Bullwinkle on TV," she replied without hesitation.

On the next page was a picture of a deer with a red nose and a holly wreath wrapped around its neck. The words below it asked, "Can you name a special deer that is popular during the winter holidays?"

I looked at Kendra, raised my eyebrows and asked, "Can *you* name that deer?"

"Yes," said my small friend, nodding sagely, "I can name her Josephine."

Tinsel Poop

The waitress (*three decades ago it was not politically incorrect to call a female waitperson a waitress*), a young woman of no more than 17 or 18, stood at the end of our table with her pencil poised. "Are you ready to order?" She asked. Then she sniffled.

Mom noticed her red-rimmed eyes. "What's the matter, dear?"

"My dog had eight pups," she began, "and I was able to give all of them away but one. I thought my dad would let me keep it, but he says I have to take it to the pound today."

"What kind of puppy is it?" asked Mom.

The waitress reached deep into her bulging apron pocket and extracted a tiny black ball of fur. "As near as we can tell, he's a cocka-pomma-peeka-poo." She half-smiled as she put the puppy in Mom's outstretched hands. "I named him Brutus."

Brutus spent the next 13 years at our house.

A small dog, his primary purpose was to streak to the front door and greet each family member as enthusiastically as if he or she was a long-lost prodigal son. Brutus took his job seriously, and bounded time after time down the stairs to the landing at the entrance, his tail just a-whirling, no matter how often each family member entered the house that day.

But during the month of December, Brutus

performed extra duties. Almost overnight, he became a class act guard dog, growling and bristling and barking whenever anyone dared to come a little too close to the presents under the Christmas tree.

"How'd you teach him to do that?" I asked Mom.

Mom smiled and said nothing.

"Come on, Mom," I asked again. "How'd you get him to 'sit and stay' right there in front of the tree?"

"See that yellow present?" she replied. "That's his, and he knows it."

"What's it got in it? Dog treats?"

"Malt Balls," said Mom. "You know, those malted milk chocolate covered candies? He's crazy about them."

"You're not supposed to give a dog chocolate," I told her.

She looked at me without expression. "*You* tell him he can't have any."

I smiled. I knew the package would suddenly "disappear" the night before Christmas. Mom loved that little mutt too much to purposely risk his health. But she didn't know Brutus was subjecting himself to another type of health hazard right before our eyes.

"CAUTION TO PET OWNERS: This product is not digestible. Consumption can cause severe gastric distress in small animals." There was no such warning on the packages of tinsel 30 years ago. And Brutus had never learned to read, anyway.

What Brutus *did* learn to do was rid the bottom of the tree of all that shiny stuff by waving his plume tail like a sky duster as he climbed in among the packages. We hoped he wasn't ingesting any of it during cleaning.

"Can you imagine trotting along behind him with a

pooper scooper after he's eaten icicles?" asked Mom.

"Maybe we could train him to poop along the edge of the driveway," I replied. "It might look like we decorated out there."

"But you *know* how he likes to sneak over to the Coleman's yard to do his business," said Mom. "They'd know whose dog it was for sure if he left a glittering calling card."

A few years later, while sitting in my own living room enjoying the music of the season and gazing at my tree, I noticed a small dark animal snaking his way in among the presents. *Uh-oh*, I thought, *the cat has found the package with the catnip in it.*

But the cat was not messing with the presents. The cat was busily stripping the tinsel from the lower branches with his mouth.

"Hey you!" I hollered from my chair. "Get out of there!" I clapped my hands sharply. The cat scampered away, fully adorned with enough tinsel to decorate a small tree of his own.

I was suddenly struck by the notion that Brutus had been reincarnated. The fact that he returned to Earth as a cat named Bubba would not have amused him, but it sure made *me* smile.

"Hey Bubba," I called, getting up to rescue him from the humiliation of going outside disguised as a foil orb, "you look like the Ghost of Christmas Past." I laughed aloud as the holiday memories of Brutus flooded my brain. "Come here, Bubba, or I'll have to change your name to 'Tinsel Poop the Second'."

Like all cats everywhere, Bubba ignored me.

CSI Donnie

At first light on Christmas day, my little seven-year-old brother Donnie looked out into our backyard.

"Oh!" he exclaimed, pointing, "Someone messed up the snow!"

Visible from Donnie's bedroom window were the impressions of what appeared to be sleigh runners and the tracks of exactly 32 reindeer hooves. He scrambled into his coat and hat and scarf and boots and mittens to get a closer look.

Once outside, Donnie scrutinized the tracks from every angle. Satisfied with their authenticity, he ran to the window where Mom and Dad and I stood watching him.

"Santa was here! Santa was here!" he shrieked. "And look—you can even see where Santa made a snow angel!" Donnie gestured to a spot in the snow where there was an obvious body imprint.

"More likely," said Mother to Father, "Santa tripped over the sleigh runners while he was stumbling around out there in the dark last night."

"It could happen," Dad agreed, "but if we'd left the porch light on, it might have scared the reindeer."

Mom nodded. "Well, it's a darn good thing Santa didn't hurt himself! I wouldn't want to have to put that kind of claim in on our homeowner's insurance."

"I agree," said Dad. "Our premiums would

probably skyrocket."

Mom smiled and took his hand. "All's well, then, and I'm very glad Santa wasn't seriously injured." She kissed him on the cheek. "Merry Christmas."

Just then a jubilant Donnie bounded up the back porch steps.

"Dad!" shouted Donnie, bursting through the door. "Dad! Guess what?" Detective Donnie held up the key ring he'd found out near the snow angel. "At the North Pole, Santa drives a Chevy truck, just like you do!"

"Give them here son," said Father, holding out his hand. "And I'll be sure to get them in the mail to him today."

Donnie laughed like crazy. "There's no mail today, Dad! It's Christmas!"

"Tomorrow then," said Dad. "First thing. Now let's get you out of your wet winter gear so you can open up some presents."

"Yea!" shouted Donnie, bouncing up and down with enthusiasm. "I can't wait to see what Santa brought me!"

"Me either," I said, leading the parade to the living room. "Me either."

Annual December 24th Pajama Party

My folks owned a state-of-the-art Kodak Brownie movie camera back in the 1960s. But to take indoor movies, the camera had to be screwed into a plate in the middle of a 16-inch metal crossbar with large spotlights mounted on both ends.

Christmas morning, it wasn't sleepiness that caused us to rub our eyes as we were filmed coming down the hallway to open our presents—it was the glare of those spotlights! We could have been playing in our bedrooms for hours before it was "time" to go out into the living room to see what Santa had brought us, but every year, there's the same squinting and eye-rubbing scene.

On Christmas Eve, Mom always let us open one present "early." I hoped every year that the one I got to open would be a book, or maybe a toy, to keep me occupied the next morning until everyone else was awake.

But no, every single year it was the same thing: *pajamas!*

Now what kid in their right mind wants to open new pajamas every single Christmas Eve? When Mother handed each of us the selected gift to unwrap, how in the world did she know which one held our nightwear? It just couldn't be coincidence!

At first I thought maybe she was stacking the gifts in a certain area under the tree to make sure all four of us got new PJs when it was time to get ready for bed. So one year I mixed up the placement of all the presents. No change. The girls still got nightgowns, the boys still got action figure designs, and it was all still flannel.

The next year I ruled out the color of the wrapping paper, since everything was wrapped in different designs. So I examined the tags of every package. Written on each tag was one of our names and a funny-looking squiggly design. Some squiggles looked like an exclamation mark with a twist. Some looked all loopy and flowery.

Two days before Christmas, I saw that there was one package for each of us with the same matching design on it. And that year, those were the very packages we got to open. It must be some kind of secret code!

Try as I might, year after year, I couldn't make any kind of sense of the squiggles. By my junior year in high school, my problem-solving skills had sharpened somewhat. Christmas Eve I asked Mom if I could be the one to select our "night before Christmas" gifts to open.

"Okay," she said slowly, "but I have to approve your choices first."

I quickly picked out all four presents. She smiled. "You know which ones, but you're not sure why, are you?"

I agreed that that was the case.

My senior year in high school I took several secretarial preparation classes. I didn't want to *be* a secretary, but I wanted to be sure my typing and other skills would serve me well in college.

Mid-December rolled around, and suddenly the Christmas code made sense. I picked up package after package from under the tree and *knew* exactly what was inside.

Smugly, I went into the kitchen and confronted my mother. "The jig's up, Mom," I told her. "You're going to have to stop writing what's inside the presents on everyone's gift tags."

She looked up from her cookie icing, tilted her head and asked, "And why's that?"

"Because..." I smiled and stole a frosted cookie from the racks. "I'm taking shorthand this year, and I'm at the top of my class."

Her eyebrows nearly hit her hairline and she jumped to her feet. *"Janet Marie!"*

There were no more squiggly marks on package tags after that day, but I still got a new nightgown to wear on my last Christmas Eve at home. Marked in bold, dark blue felt pen all across the red and green wrapping paper, it clearly said, "PJs for Jan."

And the next morning, there we all were, coming down the hallway in our new pajamas, dutifully yawning and exaggeratedly rubbing our eyes, eager to see what Santa had brought us.

Santa had brought my folks an early present that year—a new and improved camera, which no longer needed spotlights in order to film indoors.

But we rubbed our eyes anyway, for in our family, it's all about traditions.

Searching for Sinterklaas

"Mom!" hollered Ricky from the bedroom my friend Anna Marie calls her office. "Mom! What's a b-r-o-t-h-e-l?"

Anna Marie's tea splashed clear across the kitchen table as she slammed down her mug and jumped to her feet. In two bounding strides she was across the room and halfway down the hall.

I followed at a somewhat slower pace.

Nine-year-old Ricky was seated in front of the computer terminal, calmly scrolling through an Internet website.

"You know the rules!" exclaimed Anna Marie, spinning his chair around so that he faced her. "You're off the computer for a week, young man!"

"But...Mom..." protested Ricky, "I just wanted to know if Santa Claus had an e-mail address."

Anna Marie froze. I couldn't contain a strangled snicker. She shot me a 'you-try-being-a-parent' look and I bit my tongue.

"Ricky," she said softly, "please go to your room. I'll come talk to you about this in a few minutes."

Ricky left without further argument while Anna Marie and I hastily pulled chairs up to the computer table. She pulled down the 'History' window in the menu bar. Sure enough, Ricky had attempted to access information on Santa Claus. He had then followed over a dozen links to the sites exploring the history of Saint Nicholas.

"Listen to this," said Anna Marie, as she paraphrased the text on the first screen. "The Feast of Saint Nicholas, primarily a European children's festival, is celebrated on December 6, the anniversary of the day he died in the early 300s."

"That's not going to sell a whole lot of greeting cards," I interjected.

She ignored me. "In some countries, children fill their shoes with straw and carrots for Saint Nicholas' horse on the night of December 5th. In the morning, they find the straw and carrots replaced by small toys and cookies if they've been good and a whipping rod if they've been naughty.

"The Dutch brought the festival to America during the 1600s, and in the 1800s the figure of Saint Nicholas became Santa Claus."

"Go on."

"That's all the information at this site." Anna Marie pressed the button labeled 'back' and selected another entry. "Here we go. Nicholas was Bishop of Myra, a town in present-day Turkey."

"Saint Nick came from Turkey? Aren't you getting him confused with Saint Thanksgiving?"

"Do you want me to continue or not?" asked Anna Marie.

"By all means, continue—we haven't gotten to the part about the brothel yet."

Anna Marie read on: "Nicholas had an affluent background. When he was still a young man he heard of an honorable family that had fallen into poverty. The family had three daughters, who were unable to marry because their father was too poor to offer a dowry. In desperation, the father resolved to deliver his daughters to a brothel."

"Was the father's real name 'Daddy Dearest'?"

"*Anyway,*" said Anna Marie reading on, "Nicholas came up with a scheme to assist the family. He tossed three packets of money through the daughters' bedroom window one night. The money was a sufficient dowry for the three daughters. The tradition of giving gifts on Christmas morning stems from Nicholas' act of charity."

"Hold on a minute," I said. "Exactly what does all this have to do with Christmas?"

"I cannot be responsible for the validity of information found on the Internet," said Anna Marie. "Let's check another site.

"This one says that in much of Europe, men in bishops' robes pose as Saint Nicholas on December 6, examine children on their prayers, urge them to be good, and give them gifts."

"December 6 is not Christmas." I took control of the computer mouse and accessed another entry.

Anna Marie continued reading aloud over my shoulder. "Sinterklaas is Dutch for Saint Nicholas. Dutch immigrants founded the colony of New Amsterdam, which, in 1664, became New York. Sinterklaas became Santa Claus in America. After several decades, Christian society found it more appropriate to bring this 'children's festival' closer to that of the birth of the Infant Jesus. Saint Nicholas henceforth made his rounds to Christian families during the night of December 24." She smiled. "There, are you happy now?"

"Not quite." I scanned several more sites. "Okay, here's where the chimney comes in. This version says that Saint Nicholas threw three bags of gold down the chimney of the girls destined to be sold into prostitution."

"Which reminds me," said Anna Marie with a sigh, "I guess I better go talk to Ricky."

"Guess so." I agreed. "Meantime, I'll just sit here quietly and try to keep from making lame jokes about Santa shouting 'Ho, Ho, Ho!'"

"I'd appreciate that," said Anna Marie.

Downtown Evergreens

"The City of Long Beach is lining the downtown area with six-foot evergreens," said the principal of our school, "and they'd like your classes to decorate them."

My first thought was how in the world would I be able to work another art project (*and mini-field trip*) into my already jam-packed December curriculum. My second thought was *what fun!*

Fortunately, the second thought prevailed, and I waved my hand eagerly in the air.

"How many total trees? Will each class have a tree to decorate or will they be sharing? Will there be more than one tree per class? What day do they want us there? What time? Will that count as our recess? Are they going to block off traffic for us? Will the newspaper be notified so they can take pictures? May we invite parents to come with us to help out? How much laminator film will be allotted for our decorations?"

And that's how I found myself heading up the entire project.

As it turned out, each class would have several trees to adorn. We made hundreds of construction paper "ornaments" and put green or yellow yarn through punched holes in them so we could tie them onto the trees. Green and yellow were our school colors.

I found out where each tree would be placed, and made a diagram identifying which class would be responsible for which trees. Distributing these diagrams to the teachers at a staff meeting the morning of our three-block walk "downtown," I had high hopes we could pull this off without a hitch.

Unfortunately, our 4th, 5th, and 6th graders were so excited, that by the time we all walked to the center of town, the classes were spread far and wide. Few children had any concept of the planning diagram, and few adults cared to try reining them in.

Chaos prevailed as the children joyfully skipped from tree to tree, randomly tying their art projects here and there, laughing and shouting and creating quite a stir in the small business section of town.

"At least it's not raining," one of my senior colleagues said, surveying the scene with a smile and a head shake.

"But my plan!" I cried out. "This is a disaster!"

"No," she wisely corrected me, "not a disaster, just another learning experience."

The students finally had most of the 22 trees covered with enough decorations to make them look rather festive, and I was pleased that none of my charges got hit by cars as they dashed back and forth across the street.

So what if the trees weren't done class by class? So what if they hadn't followed my plan? So what if our scheduled 30-minute excursion took up the better part of the afternoon?

The newspaper reporter scurried here and there, snapping pictures and taking down the names of some of the happiest kids on the planet that day. The spirit of the season was celebrated with reckless abandonment.

At long last, we gathered our classes together, counted noses, and started back for the school building, barely in time to board the busses for home. One of the other teachers started singing, and most of the group joined in: "City sidewalks, busy sidewalks, dressed in holiday style..."

Christmas Bells, those Christmas Bells!

"I was wondering if you'd like to help us out by being a bell-ringer," said the voice on my answering machine. I cringed, returning the call with a fully prepared list of excuses beginning with the tried and true, "I just don't have the time."

But the voice, I'll call him Dale, belonged to the Presbyterian choir director. Never underestimate the power of a Presbyterian choir director. He was gently insistent; it was obvious he was used to dealing with reluctant volunteers. "We'll practice when it's convenient to your schedule," he said. "I think we can get by with only three or four rehearsals."

"Uh, Dale? Unless you count the first 12 measures of 'Born Free' on the piano, my formal education did not include learning to play a musical instrument."

"You'll be responsible for two bells—two notes," he said. "One for each hand."

My resolve waivered.

"It'll be a lot of fun," he continued. "You'll enjoy it."

"I'll make you a deal," I compromised, "I'll come to the first practice, and when you see how hopeless I am, I won't take offense if you ask me not to come back."

At the first practice, Dale handed me the white cotton gloves and pointed out the 'A' and 'G' bells. "You won't have to make any bell changes for flats or sharps during either number."

Flats? Sharps? *Either* number? "You mean we're doing more than one song?"

Dale smiled patiently. "I wrote special arrangements for both 'Joy to the World' and 'Joseph, Dearest Joseph, Mine.'"

"I've never heard of the second one," I said honestly, "but the first one sound familiar. It starts with 'Jeremiah was a bullfrog'— right?"

He knew I was teasing him.

I took my place among the other ding-a-lings and mumbled, "My only qualification for this job is my ability to count to four."

"You only need to count to three in the second one," said one woman, "it's technically a waltz."

Small consolation, I thought, for a person who had never quite had the time or inclination to master the art of reading music.

Dale discovered that small fact a short time later. Even that did not deter him. He simply took my music and coded in the notes I was to play with two colors of felt-tipped highlighter pens.

Unfortunately, he coded the left hand pink and the right hand green. Big mistake. Living the last 18 years on the coast has subliminally influenced my brain. As any good sailor knows, it's 'red, right, returning' on the channel markers. Whenever I saw a pink note I automatically lifted my right hand instead of my left.

Undaunted, Dale re-coded all my notes blue. "Notes on the lines with the left hand, notes on the spaces with the right."

The next few minutes went by fairly well, until the

woman on my right missed a beat and failed to ring her bell. The woman on my left elbowed me.

"That wasn't one of mine," I whispered.

"Pass it on," she whispered back, with another sharp elbow jab.

At the second practice Dale tried to get fancy with us. "Accent the melody line by striking those bells a bit harder, and ring the harmonizing notes softly."

"Right." I nodded. "Uh... What's a melody line?"

By the third rehearsal I think Dale knew he'd be lucky if we all finished the song at the same time. "Remember," he said, "if you can keep from making faces and grimacing when you make a mistake, fewer people will know you've goofed up."

On performance day a whole flock of fluttering butterflies took up restless residence in my stomach. I was thankful for the skirt around the table where our music rested; it hid my trembling knees.

The church was full of familiar faces. Not only was I about to make a total fool of myself, but I was going to do it in front of a house packed with people I knew.

"God help us," I muttered as I retrieved my bells from their protective case.

"He will," said one of the other women.

And He did.

I won't go so far as to say we were perfect, but either no one in the audience was aware of our minor boo-boos and technical blunders, or no one chose to point them out to us for fear they'd be recruited for the bell choir next year.

Next year? Well, it really was kind of fun...

Toppling Christmas Trees

Okay, raise your hand if you've ever inadvertently knocked over your Christmas tree. Uh-huh, I thought so. Me too. The latest of which, quite fortunately, was *prior* to decorating the gorgeous behemoth which stood precariously in my living room for the rest of the holiday season.

I'm not ready to say it's my fault the tree went over in the first place. The trunk of the tree was hopelessly curved, making it totally top-heavy on one side. All I wanted was for it to stand at less than a 45-degree angle. Okay, maybe my expectations were actually a little higher than that.

But it's not my fault my tree stander-upper friends didn't fully test the solidity of the evergreen's perch before they left my home.

And I suppose the argument could be made that no sane person would be crawling underneath the tree in the first place, but someone had to water it, and that someone was me. So yes, I suppose it *is* my fault that the whole thing suddenly decided to take a nap just hours after coming into the house.

And yes, I do accept responsibility for the half gallon of water that spilled out over the carpet when it fell. There was just no way to do anything but scream and cover my head when the tree collapsed on top of me.

But the next day I got more help, and before long it

stood—tall, proud and fully decorated, a glorious sight to behold. And I'm counting fishing line and cup hooks and friends who know how to use them among my everlasting blessings.

O Tannenbaum! O Tannenbaum! Wie treu sind deine Blätter!

Out of the Mouths of Babes

The Christmas Eve church service was pretty late for a 5-year-old to attend, but my little nephew Phillip insisted he wanted to go. He solemnly promised, crossing his heart with a big, exaggerated "X," not to get cranky.

His mother, my sister, thought that keeping him up late before the "big day" might be a good way for everyone in the household to get a little extra sleep in the morning, so she agreed to take him with us.

Phillip entered the church solemnly, holding onto one of each of our hands. As we entered the sanctuary, everyone we encountered nodded and smiled to us, and especially to Phillip. Many friends said a cheery holiday hello in hushed tones. Some waved from where they sat. We found a spot for the three of us in the second pew and settled in.

Wide-eyed, Phillip watched as the story of the immaculate birth was reenacted by the older children from the Sunday School. He delighted in the children dressed as shepherds and wooly sheep, and a small gasp escaped him as the angels, sporting glittering halos, gathered around the manger.

The moving ceremony concluded with the lighting of individual candles. Row by row, the ushers lit the first person's candle, and the flame was carefully passed along. My sister and I kept a sharp eye on Phillip as he reverently held his candle upright with both his little hands.

The lights were dimmed, and we all stood as one, preparing to sing an a cappella rendition of "Silent Night." Just one chord was struck on the organ to signal the start of this final hymn.

Deeply moved by the spirit of the evening, and awed by flickering of so many candles, at the sound of the organ Phillip quickly opened his mouth and burst into song as only a jubilant 5-year-old can do: "Happy Birthday to you…"

The congregation stifled their laughter and quickly joined him, singing, "Happy Birthday, dear Jesus…"

And that would have been a perfectly suitable ending to this story, had Phillip not capped it by tugging insistently at my sleeve as the song's conclusion. "Jannie," he loudly whispered. "Jannie, does Jesus have the same birthday as Santa Claus?"

A woman in the pew in front of us turned around and smiled. She crouched down to Phillip's level, patted his hand and whispered back, "Yes he does, Phillip. He most certainly does!"

Seasoning's Greetings

"You remember that story you always tell about how your Dad lost the band-aid off his finger while he was stuffing the Christmas turkey?" asked my friend Anna Marie during one year's holiday dinner at her house.

I paused with my fork half way to my mouth. We'd never found that particular missing band-aid. What, exactly, was she trying to tell me here?

"Well," Anna Marie continued, "I know for a fact that I started off with two paper seasoning packets in the dressing mix, but now I can only account for one."

Everyone at the table exhaled at the same time, resulting in the necessity of relighting the centerpiece candles. Lost seasoning packet? No problem! Dad's band-aid, however, was a whole 'nother story...

I smiled at the memory. "It's something we'll laugh about later," Dad had told me. Dad had been right. We've laughed about it for over 30 years now, and each year there are new faces at the Christmas dinner table who haven't heard the story told, and so it is repeated, once again, for posterity.

Every family has their share of semi-disastrous culinary experiences, like accidentally using baking powder instead of baking soda; substituting semi-sweet baking chocolate for Nestle's morsels; leaving an apple pie to cool on the back porch and later discovering the

36

neighbor's standard poodle has made short work of it.

Good thing Mom had placed her legendary "Chocolate Surprise Pie" on the rack above the refrigerator to set that Christmas. She always made a big deal out of her chocolate pudding pie, and handled it with utmost care.

Early on the morning of the feast (*she waited till the last minute so the crust would stay flaky*), Mom mixed up the pie dough. It was usually my job to keep stirring the pudding in the double boiler, making sure it didn't stick to the bottom of the pan. There'd be all heck to pay if the pudding scorched, and I made darn sure it didn't happen on *my* watch.

Mom rolled out the crust to a uniform thickness, deftly crimped the edges around the glass pie plate, and poked numerous small holes in the dough with a fork so it wouldn't bubble up while baking. Then she stood guard at the oven door, watching the crust turn a light, golden amber.

"Don't look," she'd tell me, as if I didn't know what she was up to. "I'm going to put a surprise in the bottom of the pie."

Mom's 'surprise' was always a layer of thinly-sliced bananas, which was carefully concealed beneath her expert signature swirling pattern on the top of the pudding.

"Okay, who wants chocolate pie?" Mom joyfully asked after dinner the year the 60-plus pound poodle absconded with any choice in the matter of dessert.

"Ooooh," said my slightly-more-sarcastic-than-droll brother John, "is it..." he paused for effect, "could it possibly be..." His eyes got bigger as he exaggerated his excitement. "Did you have time to make us a *chocolate surprise pie?*"

Mother shot him a look. "Do you want some pie or not?"

John assented, and Mom gave him the first piece. Without examination, he took a big bite. Mother hovered just close enough to his chair to arouse my suspicions.

"Hey!" exclaimed a genuinely surprised John with his mouth still full. "What'd you put in the bottom of this pie?"

"*Surprise!*" shouted Mom, gleefully clapping her hands. "I gotcha!" She looked proud as a strutting peacock. "I put mini-marshmallows in the bottom this year! I gotcha, fair and square!"

Good friends, good food, good stories. What would the holidays be without them?

"I just feel so foolish," said Anna Marie a few years ago. "I mean, what kind of mother am I? I don't often manage to pull off a big sit-down dinner for my family and friends, and when I do, I have to admit that not only did I not make the dressing totally from scratch, but I misplaced one of the packets of seasoning." She sighed and shook her head.

"Don't feel bad, Mom," said Anna Marie's son little Ricky (*who frequently reminds me that he was 13 at the time, and I simply MUST stop calling him little Ricky in my stories*), "you may never be Martha Stewart, but you can always be a Spice Girl."

Now *there's* a kid imbued with the spirit of the seasonings!

Oh, Fudge!

Judy unceremoniously plopped herself down on the steps between my dining and living rooms and absentmindedly scratched behind the cat's eager ears.

"Dad's passing the torch." She sighed. "So I guess it's up to me."

I flipped on the Christmas tree lights, sat on the step next to her, and waited patiently. (*Hey, I know it's not my strong suit, but I did the best I could.*)

"For the past 25 years," Judy continued, "Dad's been the one to make the holiday fudge for the whole family." She sighed again. "But now his health is too poor for him to do that."

"So you've been making fudge?" I prompted her.

"Sort of."

"Sort of? How do you 'sort of' make fudge?"

"Well—" Judy smiled at the thought. "So far I've learned that you have to cook fudge a lot longer than you cook soup."

I barely managed to stifle a grin. "How long?"

"Thirty-seven minutes a batch seems to come out about right."

"Yep." I nodded. "That's a little longer than soup."

We contemplated the sparkling tinsel and tree lights for a moment, then I broke our companionable silence. "Are you using a candy thermometer?"

"I am now."

If this wasn't one of the oddest conversations I'd ever had! I'm a fine one to give culinary advice! I wouldn't recognize a candy thermometer if it bit me in the butt, but it seemed like a reasonable thing to say at the time.

Judy brightened. "I found the cutest little fudge tins to pack it in." She frowned. "But then I decided I had to buy round cooling pans because it's hard to fit square fudge in a round tin."

Her accounting of the entire process (*or was that ordeal?*) was beginning to sound like a good news/bad news comedy routine.

"The pans are just the perfect size." She beamed, then looked pensive. "Do you think it's okay if I don't cut the fudge into pieces before I ship it?"

I assumed her question was rhetorical.

"When I transfer the round two-inch-thick slab of fudge to the tin it looks so cool. I've never seen anything like it. It looks like a beautiful big brown frisbee."

"Don't drop it on you toe," I warned her, "you could hurt yourself." I laughed. "I imagine a giant cow patty like that could kill a cat—" I looked at the animal sprawled between us. "Or small children—"

"Death by chocolate." Judy giggled.

"I can see the headlines now," I snickered, "Fudgemaker's Frisbee Flattens Family."

"I wonder what that fudge actually weighs," mused Judy.

"You'll find out when you mail it if it's worth all the time, trouble and postage," I told her. "What all goes into your sweet confection?"

"It's a very well-kept old family secret," she began,

"but I'll share it with you. You start with four cups of sugar, one cup of cocoa, two cups of evaporated milk…"

"*Four cups of sugar?!*" I interrupted her recipe recital. "Four cups is a *quart*! You put a *quart* of sugar and a pint of milk in each batch?!"

Judy nodded.

I figured aloud: "As a general rule, a pint's a pound. So there's roughly two pounds of sugar, one pound of milk and a half a pound of cocoa in each batch. That's a 3 1/2 pound frisbee if you don't add any nuts to it."

"I make some with nuts," she said, "but the tin lids won't go on if I put the whole batch in one pan." She smiled. "Discovered that little fact by trial and error. I've been eating my mistakes."

I thought about the cost of the ingredients, the cooling pans, the tins, the postage, and the enormous amount of time and energy involved. "You know," I suggested softly, "Anna Lena's makes several varieties of very good fudge. And they'll ship it for you, too."

Judy glared at me. "It's a labor of love."

"Of course it is," I replied. "I understand completely. You spend days and days and days making fudge from an old family recipe which is later passed down through the generations just like my great Aunt Flora's fruitcake."

Judy looked puzzled. "I'm confused," she said. "Are you referring to the recipe or the actual fruitcake being handed down?"

I smiled and gazed at the twinkling behemoth in the living room. "Now *that*, my dear friend, is one well-kept old family secret I'm *not* willing to share!"

Happy HanChrisKwanadan!

"Par-ty! Par-ty! Par-ty!" I chanted as I danced a modified jig around my rec room a few years ago.

"Whoa, girl!" said Anna Marie, laughing. "Aren't you the one who annually goes into a state of semi-hibernation as the days grow shorter?"

Winded, I plopped into the recliner and kicked out the footrest. "Yep. You're looking at the very same woman who's been known to pull the bed covers up over her head late winter afternoons just as soon as the sun goes down."

"So where'd all this new-found energy come from?"

I smiled. "Ever know me to pass up a party?"

"Not in this lifetime…"

"Well," I continued, "a quick check of the planetary alignment and you can see for yourself that to maintain my party animal image I'll have no time for sleep this month." I handed her my calendar/planner.

"Wow," said Anna Marie. "I didn't even know some of these holidays existed."

"But did you know," I asked her, "that the word 'holiday' originates from the Middle Ages when 'holy days' were first observed as a break from days of warfare?"

"Obviously they never had my ex in-laws over for Thanksgiving dinner."

I chose (*as I often do when I'm upstaged by a terrific*

punch line I wished I'd thought of myself) to ignore her.

"The secret of a full social calendar," I elaborated, "is to not limit oneself to any specific culture or religion. By being truly ecumenical, I can find reason to celebrate every single day of the darkest month of the year and joyfully keep myself from falling into the moody blue abyss of wintertime depression, also known as S.A.D."

"S.A.D.?" queried Anna Marie.

"Seasonal Affective Disorder. The absence of sunlight makes sufferers like me terribly lethargic, hence the hibernation ruse. But the way the calendar is set up this year, all the twinkling tree lights and converging candles ought to help keep our collective attitudes quite well-adjusted."

"Couldn't you just get a sunlamp?"

"Got one. But it's not the same. Sunlamping is such a solitary pastime."

"You could go south for the winter. Lots of people from around here spend a good part of the winter in Mexico."

"It's too expensive, I don't speak Spanish, and you seem to forget that I have a job here that requires my attendance."

"Well for me," sighed Anna Marie, "Christmas is almost more than I can handle." She paused, perusing the list I'd handed her. "I have several Jewish friends, so I pretty much know about Hanukkah, and there's been a lot on the news recently about Kwanzaa, but what's Ramadan?"

"Ramadan is the ninth month of the Islamic calendar. Muslims fast from sunrise to sunset during the 29 days of Ramadan, but at night the amusement parks are open and a big meal is shared. It honors the time when the Koran, the holy book of Islam, was given to the prophet Muhammed. This year Ramadan begins on December 31st."

"I kind of like that idea," she said. "Fasting during the day would be an excellent way to get a jump-start on a January diet."

"Next year Ramadan begins on December 20th."

"Oh."

Anna Marie scanned through the list a second time. "Let's see… Advent began the Sunday after Thanksgiving. The Feast of St. Nicholas was December 6th. The winter solstice, complete with a scheduled three-day yule log burning, is December 22nd. Hanukkah begins at sundown December 23rd this year.

"Then there's Christmas Eve and, of course, Christmas Day. Kwanzaa covers the seven days from the 26th through January 1st, which is New Year's Day. Ramadan lasts a full month, ending with a three-day gift-giving celebration called Id-al-Fitr.

"The Feast of the Three Kings, otherwise known as the Epiphany, otherwise known as the 12th day of the 12 Days of Christmas, culminates on January 6th… Do these holidays *always* line up like this?"

"Nope." I shook my head. "This year's special. This year we're blaming it all on El Nino."

"El Nino?"

"Why not? Everything else this year has been blamed on El Nino."

"Because," said Anna Marie, "I think your explanation heavily favors the Christians."

"I don't get it."

Anna Marie enjoyed watching me squirm before she supplied the missing link to my holiday edification. "In parts of Mexico," she explained, "the Christmas gift-giver is 'El Nino Jesus,' which in English means 'The Infant Jesus'. The Infant, El Nino, arrives in the wintertime."

Once again, Anna Marie bests me in semantics. Happy Holydays everyone. Party hearty.

All or Nothing

My ultimate Christmas coup came at the very last minute of childhood. I was 16. The first week of December I made my all-or-nothing proclamation: "If I can't have a car for Christmas, then I don't want anything."

Dad's eyebrows flew toward his hairline. "A car?"

The element of surprise was on my side. Dad was caught unprepared to do battle with a tactically terroristic teen.

I gave him my well-thought-out list of reasons why buying me a car for Christmas would be the most practical, rational, and loving thing he would do in his entire lifetime. I could run errands for Mom, chauffeur my younger siblings, and have more time to do my homework by avoiding the long and winding bus ride to and from school.

"Your grandparents didn't hand me a car when I was your age," he began.

"Don't you want me to have more than you had when you were a kid?" I countered.

"Who'll put gas in it?"

"I'll use my babysitting money."

"What about insurance?

"I have better than a B grade-point average. There's a big discount for teen drivers with good grades."

"Do you happen to know what a decent used car

costs?"

"There's a light blue '66 Mustang with a 289 V-8 engine over on the lot on 196th that seems to be priced very reasonably."

"*A Mustang!*" The cords on his neck threatened to explode.

Oops. Strategic error. I retreated to my bedroom to do my homework and plan my next move.

Throughout Advent I tried to chip away at Dad's steadfast resistance. Mom suggested I put something else on my Christmas wish list. I declined. "I told you what I want," I reminded her, "and I'm every bit as stubborn as Dad is."

By Christmas Eve things looked mighty bleak. When it came time to hang our stockings, I reluctantly hung up a pair of panty hose in my traditional spot above the fireplace.

"I don't know why you're bothering," said Dad. "You said you wanted nothing for Christmas."

That evening everyone else's pile of presents under the tree grew higher and higher. A few measly gifts, all with the tags written in unmistakably childish scrawl, bore my name. This was either a very good sign, or I had just blown my entire holiday.

Around 9 o'clock Dad strolled over to the fireplace and nonchalantly dropped something into the panty hose. I shrieked and bolted for my stocking, ripping it from the hearth. Keys clattered to the floor.

Keys to the family station wagon.

In shocked disbelief, I looked at Dad. He shrugged. "I told you a month ago we couldn't afford a car," he said. "So I got you a new key ring and your own set of keys to the Chrysler." I flew from the room and down the hall to my bedroom, slamming the door. Dad had called my bluff.

A short time later Mom convinced me to be a good sport and come out from my self-imposed exile. As I begrudgingly joined the others, headlights from a vehicle pulling into our driveway scanned across the room. My youngest brother wiggled behind the Christmas tree to look out the living room window.

"It's Santa! It's Santa! It's Santa! It's Santa!" He could hardly contain himself, jumping up and down and waving his arms in excitement. "It's Santa, Jannie, and he's driving your new blue car!"

And the rest, as they say, is history.

Walnut Garland and Airplane Parts

"Aunt Jo wants to know who has the walnut garland," said Mom.

"Walnut garland?" I replied, feigning innocence. "What walnut garland?"

"Don't play coy with me," she said. "I know you have it, cause I'm the one who sent it to you last year."

She had a point there. Camouflaging the less-than-precious family heirloom inside an empty cardboard toilet paper roll, Mom then wrapped it in an expensive-looking box tied up with silver and gold ribbons.

Mom got it from Aunt Jo the previous year. Aunt Jo had skipped a step in the loop and shipped it back from whence it came the year before that.

"The Garland" was discovered by Great Aunt Flora among her Christmas ornaments a few decades ago. All that's left of "The Garland" are four gold-painted walnut shells glued along a 15 inch length of double-strand green yarn.

Once upon a time, some long-forgotten ancestor of ours carefully cracked dozens of walnuts open and removed the nutmeats, leaving the halves of the shells intact. The shells were hand-painted gold, and the two sides glued back together straddling the yarn at approximately one-inch intervals. The finished garland was used to decorate the Christmas tree.

"I'm sure someone will want to hang onto this,"

Great Aunt Flora had said, lovingly lifting it from the box of decorations.

I remember looking at my mother, who was looking at Aunt Jo with a peculiar expression. Aunt Jo, not in Great Aunt Flora's immediate line of vision, made a face back at Mom. Mom rolled her eyes toward the ceiling.

"This garland has been in the family a long time," continued GAF. "Now which one of you girls shall I give it to?"

"*Pat!!*" exclaimed Mom and Aunt Jo together.

"I hate to give it up," Mom hastened to explain, "but Pat's the oldest of your nieces."

"It should rightfully go to her," Aunt Jo chimed in, nodding.

Aunt Pat wasn't there to defend herself. So the worn piece of garland, not much more than enough to use for a package decoration (*not that anyone would want to*) was cleverly wrapped in tissue paper and tagged for Aunt Pat in GAF's shaky and nearly indecipherable scrawl.

The following year Aunt Jo discovered the garland inside a package under her own tree.

Mother received it the year after that, nestled between two boxes of Jiffy Cornbread Mix.

The three sisters shuffled the garland around for years, hiding it inside an empty tube of wrapping paper, or deep inside the toe of a Christmas sock. Somehow I got involved with the gift that keeps on giving and last year it came through the mail to me.

Meanwhile, my two brothers, both in their 50s, have been passing a box of model airplane parts back and forth since they were teen-agers. Together they had built a gas-powered airplane that made a hellacious amount of noise as it flew circles around them, guided by double-fisted fishing line controls.

When the plane crashed and burned (*figuratively speaking*) and presumably beyond repair, the boys boxed up the pieces to work on some other day. But 'some other day' has a way of slipping right through your fingers, and the plane was doomed never to see quality airtime again.

The boys, however, have kept their aerodynamic dreams alive. They don't find it necessary to wait for December to 'pass the parts.' The slightly-larger-than-shoebox carton has shown up in an unlocked car, left on porch steps, and hidden in the bottom of their kid's overnight bag all in the same year.

By definition, a tradition is the handing down of an inherited, established, or customary pattern of thought, action or behavior. A legacy is a gift received from an ancestor or predecessor. Nowhere in my dictionary do I see any mention of walnut garland or airplane parts.

Yet for just a moment between Thanksgiving and Christmas, I pause to think fondly of GAF, and of Aunt Pat, who have now both gone on to their rewards. I stop to think of the good times we shared, and I know I am blessed to have in my possession a short hunk of golden shells glued to green yarn as a tangible, if less-than-elegant, monument to those memories.

But I'm not keeping it. No way am I going to be stuck with our family's equivalent of the 'Old Maid.' This is one torch that begs to be passed!

Presents Under the Tree

Each Christmas, Mom insists upon giving presents to my cat Bubba. She wraps a myriad of silly little gifts and puts ribbons and bows and tags on them, just as if the cat cares. But he seems to enjoy the fluffy little toys on strings and the plastic balls with bells inside. And just like a kid, sometimes he plays with the bows and paper almost as long as he plays with the toys.

Of all the gifts, however, I think he especially looks forward to receiving the traditional little cans of cat food Mom always tries to disguise by wrapping them in various colors of paper. She knows I don't normally give my cat canned food, but since Mom always finds a coupon she can use, and I'm the only kid who has a cat, Bubba is the obvious recipient.

A few days before Christmas last year, Bubba and I had a picnic dinner in the living room. With the twinkling tree lights as the backdrop, I opened him a can of Fancy Feast and emptied it onto a cut-glass saucer. He dined on a placemat decorated with a pretty Christmas design while I sat beside him on the floor and ate a tasty turkey and dressing microwave meal.

We enjoyed our quality time so much that the following night I repeated the experience. Bubba was thrilled! He gobbled up his dinner in no time flat and nosed around the packages to see if there might be more gourmet meals tucked away for him.

But the next night I had other plans, and for several days he got only his regular dry cat food in his regular bowl at its regular place. On Christmas Eve, however, I again reached under the tree to get out another ribbon-tied can. Imagine my surprise, *and dismay!* to discover Bubba had brought his own special little offering to the banquet table.

In among the gifts, I found irrefutable evidence that on the night before Christmas, at least at my house, "Not a creature was stirring, not even a mouse."

Welcome to Tinsel Town

If Norman Rockwell could have added sounds and smells to the scenes he painted, he would have loved spending the holiday season at my house. Window lights twinkled in time to carols playing on the stereo, the fire crackled happily in the woodstove, and the aromas of evergreen and cinnamon filled the air.

Warmed, no doubt, more by the hot spiced wassail than the fire, my former student Scott, now a grown young man in his mid-thirties, volunteered to put the tinsel on the top portion of my 12-foot Christmas tree.

I readily accepted his offer, but first I insisted we discuss how tinsel should be applied. I heard my old teacher voice kick into automatic pilot.

"You do not," I explained, "hang it in great bunches and globs. Neither do you attempt to reverse the motor on the vacuum cleaner and blow the icicles onto the tree. And you most certainly do not toss it high into the overhead ceiling fan with the hope it will be distributed evenly on the branches."

I demonstrated proper technique. "Tinsel is like rain," I further pontificated, "the drops falling softly toward the earth, reflecting little rainbows among the colored lights."

The look Scott gave me clearly told me I was overdoing it, so before he could change his mind about helping out, I abruptly ended the lesson.

After positioning the ladder and handing him the first of the 24 boxes of icicles intended to embellish the tree, I retreated to the kitchen to finish up some last minute candy-making. I had completed two—or was it three?—batches of microwaved cashew bark when I realized it was awfully quiet in the other part of the house.

Holy St. Nick!

While the strains of "Silver Bells" filled the air, Scott had transformed my living room into one garishly glistening sea of gaudiness. My domestic quarters looked like the aftermath of an explosion at the Reynold's aluminum factory!

Where *wasn't* there tinsel?

Strands of the silver stuff hung from the potted plants, the drapes, the lamps, the pictures on the wall, and the ears of most of my teddy bears. Tinsel was crammed into the fingers of gloves, the toes of shoes, inside the lidded candy dish, under the couch cushions, and between the pages of the books on the coffee table.

Carefully, ever so carefully, Scott had managed to hang tinsel from the cobwebs high in the beamed ceiling, along the strands of lights that outlined the doorway arches, and on the Casa Blanca fan that turned slowly overhead.

He'd thought of everything; even the ladder he perched upon was covered with icicles. Most amazingly, the tree had somehow managed to get a few strands properly placed upon its branches.

"I had a little left over." Scott grinned, and his dimples made him look just like the impish 10-year-old kid he'd been in class.

What could I do?

For starters, I did an impersonation of a guppy; my eyes got big and round, and my mouth opened and closed several times without a single sound coming out. And then I did something that surprised even me—I erupted into fits of uncontrollable laughter.

Scott, undoubtedly relieved by my reaction, climbed down from the ladder and joined me in the doorway.

"Merry Christmas," he said, draping tinsel from the corner of my eyeglasses.

Yes, I thought, as I wiped away the tears of mirth, this is what the holiday season is really all about: laughter and friendship and good times to be remembered. I had all the next day to figure out how I was going to get the house back in order before company arrived.

"Merry Christmas," I replied.

Ninja Santas

On "Black Friday," the official start to holiday shopping season, I was working the Grange Bazaar. To set the tone, I wore a bright holiday hat and a pair of festive metal star-shaped Santa earrings.

When a former student of mine came in, I was delighted to see her, and gave her a big, happy hug. She immediately flinched and pulled away.

"Ms. B.! You're wearing Ninja Santas on your ears!"

Fortunately, I hadn't punctured her, and she sat down for a nice long chat about her current college challenges. I'm always happy to see "my children" succeed, and I enjoy watching them evolve into the amazing adults I predicted they would become.

At the end of our conversation, she stood to leave, but put both hands up to fend me off. "I don't want to get near those crazy earrings again," she said with a laugh.

I gently hugged her anyway, being mindful of the potential Weapons of Mass Destruction hanging from my ear lobes.

Relating this story to a frazzled girlfriend of mine later that day when she returned, exhausted, from the "crazed and kamikaze world of bargain hunting," she suggested I might wear them in self-defense as I finished my own holiday shopping.

I'm not the 4 a.m. Warrior Shopper type myself, but I did offer to lend her my earrings.

A Divine Christmas Tradition

A picture-perfect Christmas Eve afternoon—carols drifting softly from the stereo, tree lights twinkling, the neighbors' kids gathered to play Monopoly in the rec room. A slow all-day drizzle settled in over the Pacific Northwest.

Dad came upstairs from working on his car in the garage.

"Whaddya say you and I try making some divinity?" he asked me while reaching for the double boiler.

"Uh-oh," said Mom. "You're going to attempt making divinity while it's raining?" She got her purse and coat from the hall closet. "I think I'll just run to the store for a few last-minute groceries. I'll be back in an hour or so."

Dad laughed as she backed the car out of the driveway. "Happens every year," he mused.

"Why is that?" I asked.

"Oh, years ago, when your mother and I were newly married, we thought it would be nice to start a family Christmas tradition. We decided to make divinity together one damp Christmas Eve."

"Just like you and me today, right?"

"Well, not exactly. You see, we were pretty young and neither of us really knew how to make the stuff. We didn't have a candy thermometer, and we didn't even have a clue what 'hard ball stage' meant."

"So what happened?"

"Let's just say it's a miracle we didn't burn the house down."

"Oh, Dad, you're exaggerating."

"Maybe," he admitted, "but maybe not."

I soon finished chopping the walnuts, leaned my elbows on the counter, and watched him pour the cooked corn syrup over the whipped egg whites. In just minutes, we set the light and fluffy candy aside to cool. Then Dad started a second batch.

"Don't you think we've made enough?" I asked.

Dad didn't answer.

"Dad! Wait! You're not even using the thermometer! You're sure to ruin it! It won't set up!"

He smiled. "You just don't understand yet about traditions."

Mom arrived home as I was cutting the first divinity into one-inch squares, placing half a maraschino cherry atop each piece.

"I'm home," she called out. "And I brought the chocolate ice cream."

"Chocolate ice cream?" I asked, taking the grocery sack from her.

"Sure," said Mom. "We'll need something to pour the ruined divinity over."

"But Mom, how did you know?"

Mom laughed. "Your dad always gets too anxious about his candy making. The first batch he makes never sets up, so we pour it over ice cream."

"The *first* batch?" I asked incredulously, looking quickly at Dad, who was busying himself with the dishes.

"It's kind of a tradition," said Mom. "And after a few years everyone in the house learned to just get out of the way till it's over." She turned to put the ice cream in the freezer.

Catching my eye, Dad shook his head, placed a finger to his lips, and winked.

Perle Mesta Lives!

Someone once asked me if I aimed to be the Perle Mesta of the West Coast. Of course, I had to immediately google Perle Mesta before I could respond appropriately.

In case you didn't know either, Perle Mesta was most noted for her parties, which included senators, congressmen, cabinet secretaries and other luminaries in bipartisan soirées of high-class glamour. An invitation to one of her parties was a sure sign that one had reached the inner circle of Washington political society.

Well, when you put it that way, then yes, I *do* aim to emulate Mrs. Mesta. Once a year I bring together all my various assorted and sundry groups for one big holiday shindig. I have a piano player come in from Seattle, and my writer friends, theater friends, church friends, school friends, neighbors and an eclectic assortment of 'other' friends gather around the spinet to belt out a few Christmas carols in my rec room.

As my minister once remarked, "Everyone at this party is so well-versed... But none of them are talking about the same thing!"

That's the way I like it. Different strokes for different folks, all brought together to celebrate the season. Peace on earth, goodwill to all, means *ALL*— from every walk of life, from every continent and every country, and even from both ends of the peninsula.

Let the party begin!

A Slightly Hypothermic Christmas Eve

"It's a cute outfit, Syl," said Anna Marie, "but I still think it's a dumb idea."

"That's because you've got absolutely no imagination," replied Sylvia. She primped in front of the full-length mirror, turning this way and that, admiring herself from every angle.

"At least I have a modicum of humility," said Anna Marie under her breath.

"I heard that."

"Of course you did," said Anna Marie, helping herself to another cup of coffee. "You have selective hearing. You only hear exactly what you want to hear."

Sylvia shot "the look" at her best friend. She fluffed the white fur accentuating the cleavage and along the very short hem. She checked for the umpteenth time to make sure her black garter belt wasn't showing. "You've gotta admit it—I'm adorable."

Anna Marie nearly choked on her drink. "Yeah, yeah, whatever, you're adorable."

"Come on, say it like you mean it."

"Okay, fine. That's the cutest, sexiest, most adorable, seductive, altogether raunchy and totally slutty Santa's Little Helper costume I've ever seen."

Sylvia beamed. "Now, *that's* more like it!"

"But I still think it's a dumb idea."

"What's so dumb about it?"

"Well, let me be sure I've got it straight," replied Anna Marie. "You want me to drive you to Bill's house tonight, just before he gets home from work, and leave you on his front porch, dressed like this."

"Yep, that's the plan," said Syl. "I don't want him to be tipped off by seeing my car parked in his driveway."

"What if you freeze to death before he gets home?"

"Bill's the most punctual guy I know," said Sylvia. "You can set a watch by his routine. He gets off work at 5:00, and by 5:20, he's pulling into the driveway. And besides," she continued with a sly smile, "I'll have this to keep me warm." She proudly unrolled the biggest red and white Christmas stocking Anna Marie had ever seen. "BILL" was embroidered across the top in letters almost a foot high.

"Wowza," said Anna Marie. "Where'd you get something like that?"

"On eBay, of course."

"Of course."

"So when you drop me off, I'll just snuggle into this stocking and be standing on the porch waiting for him. It's a masterpiece of an idea."

"If you say so," replied Anna Marie.

"I say so." Sylvia took a quick look at the clock on the wall. "It's almost show time," she said. "Just one more quick trip to the bathroom and I'll be all set."

Anna Marie pulled on her warm ski jacket and flipped up the hood. "You mind if I take the last bit of coffee?" she called out.

"Go right ahead," answered Syl from the bathroom. "I'm sure I'll be staying at Bill's house tonight, so flip the pot off, will you?"

Anna Marie did as she was told and gathered up her purse and car keys. Sylvia joined her in the kitchen with the sleeping bag stocking bootie draped over her arm. "Where's your coat?" asked Anna Marie.

"Don't need one," replied Sylvia, slipping into a pair of scarlet stilettos and donning a furry Santa hat to complete her outfit. "I'll only be outside for a few minutes, and after that, I guarantee that Bill will be keeping me toasty warm the rest of the night."

"Braggart," muttered Anna Marie.

"Why do you always think I can't hear you?"

"Why do you always think I don't want you to hear me?" retorted Anna Marie.

On the short drive to Bill's house, she popped a holiday music CD into the car player and turned the volume up. It was a great time of year, and she loved singing the familiar carols. By the time they arrived, Anna Marie was almost ready to concede that Sylvia's plan was a wonderfully romantic gesture.

As soon as the car came to a stop, Sylvia hopped out and scurried toward the porch. A light dusting of snow covered the walkway, and she had watch where she placed her feet. "Thank you!" Syl waved her free hand as she shivered in the chill. "I'll call you tomorrow!"

Anna Marie just shook her head and smiled. Sylvia's exploits could fill a large book. Her *successful* exploits would fill a significantly smaller volume. She tooted the horn as she drove away and conceded she might actually need a little more of Syl's holiday attitude. She'd heard the local theater was playing the original "Miracle on 34th Street," and decided to go check it out.

Meanwhile, Sylvia struggled to pull the fleece

stocking up around her bare shoulders. It wasn't quite long enough, even when she hunched down a little. *Damn*, she thought, *it's a lot colder than I imagined*. She comforted herself by the fact that it was already quarter after five. Bill would be home in a matter of minutes. She smiled as she pictured the look on his face.

At 5:45 Sylvia's teeth began to chatter.

Across town, Bill decided to have the jewelry store clerk wrap the gift he had finally selected. He was sure Syl would love the necklace, but he didn't have the time, or the necessary skill, to go home and wrap it himself. He wanted to surprise her with it under the mistletoe at her place this evening.

"You know," said the clerk, "you just made it just under the wire. We were going to close early, on account of tonight being Christmas Eve and all."

Bill smiled sheepishly. "What can I say?" He grinned. "I'm a guy."

"Poor excuse," admonished the female clerk.

"Only excuse I've got," laughed Bill. He nodded his head toward a half dozen other male shoppers still agonizing over the jewelry display cases. "And apparently I'm not the only one." He was feeling lighthearted and joyful and would have burst into song if there'd been any music playing.

He left the store with his small, precious package and decided on the spur of the moment to make an additional quick stop for a bottle of champagne. Sylvia loved champagne. And Bill particularly liked the way she giggled when the bubbles tickled her nose.

By the time he made his wine selection, it was a little after six. Instead of going home to shower and change, as originally planned, he drove straight to Syl's house. Her car was in the driveway, but no lights were on. He knocked on the front door. No answer. He dialed her cell phone and heard it ring inside the house.

With growing concern, he went around the back of the house and found the key she left there "for emergencies." Bill entered the back door and hurried through the house, flipping on all the lights and calling her name. He located her cell phone sitting on the credenza next to her purse. *Where was Syl if her purse was here?* Bill's heart pounded in his chest.

Sylvia was now huddled in a ball on Bill's porch, the stocking pulled completely over her head. She breathed on her hands and rubbed them vigorously on her legs, trying to warm them but careful not to put a run in her sheer black nylons. Shivering uncontrollably, she wondered what time it was, and chastised herself for leaving her phone behind.

Peering out from the top of the stocking, Sylvia could see the porch light on at a neighboring house a few hundred yards down the road. She weighed the pros and cons of abandoning her wrap and making a dash for it in her skimpy costume. She could live through the humiliation, but since she could not honestly tell if anyone was home, she decided to stay put. She couldn't imagine dashing to the neighboring house *and back* in her red high heels.

Bill sat down to think. *Should he call the police?* No. He'd call her best friend first. He picked up Syl's phone and saw Anna Marie's number was the last one called. He pressed the button, and heard it go straight to voice mail. *Now what?* He paced for a few more minutes before it dawned on him that Syl and Anna Marie might be somewhere together. That would explain Syl's car being at home, *but her purse?*

Don't panic, he told himself. Don't panic. He dialed his home phone number to check his messages. Nothing. Bill pulled the gift box from his jacket pocket and eyed it lovingly. "Where are you, Syl?"

At 6:30 Bill decided he'd be better off waiting at home. He pulled into his driveway just in time to see something resembling a giant red and white sleeping bag all tangled up and rolling in the snow across his lawn. He quickly parked the car and cautiously approached it.

Syl's nearly blue nose emerged from the top of the sock. "*Help,*" she whimpered.

Bill restrained himself from making a comment about how she'd fallen and couldn't get up. He also wisely fought back any trace of laughter. "Is there room in there for us both," he asked her with a straight face, "or would you like to come inside?"

Without waiting for a response, he gathered her up, bag and all, and carried her toward the house. He had a feeling it was going to take a little more than a bottle of champagne to get her warm again.

Sylvia put her arms around his neck. "M-M-M-Merry Chr-Chri-Christmas B-B-Bill...."

Bill gently kissed the top of her head. "Merry Christmas, my little snow bunny."

Twinkling Christmas Carols

Ocean Park residents Bob and Mary love Christmas. And Bob also loves fiddling with MacIntosh computers. Put the two ideas together and what you get is an amazing display Christmas lights programmed to dance and gyrate to upbeat seasonal songs.

It's a tradition in my house to drive over to Bob and Mary's at least once each December to sit in my car in their driveway and enjoy the show. By tuning the car radio to the specified station, it's like being at an old-time drive-in theater.

I think Bob has a special fondness for the music of the Trans-Siberian Orchestra. The pulsating Christmas lights intricately follow the rhythm and beat of such tunes as "Wizards in Winter" and "Carol of the Bells."

The amazing light show has an energy that feels almost alive. If you're old enough to remember the 60s, the word psychedelic aptly fits the performance. It makes you want to get out of your car and move to the music. I've never before wanted to boogie to Christmas carols, but after seeing Bob's free show, I'm having second thoughts.

And speaking of "free," there's a container out front of Bob and Mary's home for donations to the South Pacific County Humane Society. Donations for that cause are happily accepted; it's their way of passing on the love.

So when you're feeling a little overwhelmed by the abundance of "have to" activities of the season, put this one on your "want to" list. It's the best way I've found to rejuvenate myself, and once-again delight in the true spirit of Christmas.

And if you don't live anywhere near Ocean Park? Well then, feel free to start your own music and light show. I'm sure there's room enough on the planet for a few more. Meanwhile, I'll just count my blessings I live so close to the best single-home coordinated sound and light Christmas display I've ever seen.

Thank you, Bob and Mary!

The Last (Christmas) Supper

Every family has a black sheep. Our lives on "the Eastside." I call him the Bellevue Brother.

For those non-natives of the Pacific Northwest, Bellevue is located on the eastern shore of Lake Washington, and is affectionately referred to as the gateway to Nordstrom. Only a place like Bellevue would boast a grocery store featuring valet parking and seven brands of phyllo dough.

A few years ago the Bellevue Brother (BB) announced that he would like the family Christmas dinner held at his home. He and his wife had recently moved into a small, five bedroom, three-story, quadruple-garage house, and were anxious to have everyone over to see it.

I had a few reservations about this right from the get-go. For starters, my salary is nowhere near a six-figured income, and I don't drive a BMW, Audi or Lexus.

"That's okay, Sis," BB told me, "you can park in the overflow lot down the street."

I arrived fashionably on time. My sister-in-law was not yet dressed. "Come on upstairs," she called.

I noted on my way up that the spiral banister was wrapped in variegated holly.

"Wow," I said upon reaching the top of the stairs, "I'd hate to bump into that in the middle of the night!"

"Don't worry," she confided, "we had our florist

clip off the points."

Of course. How silly of me.

"Wait till you see the tree he put up in the living room," she continued.

"*Who* put up the tree?"

"Our florist. Your brother and I are much too busy with our careers to spend the time decorating it ourselves."

I opened my mouth to speak, but no words came out. My sister-in-law didn't seem to notice. "It's decorated with hand-blown glass ornaments," she said, while liberally applying Vidal Sassoon hairspray. "Imported, of course."

"Imported ornaments? From what country?"

"No, not the ornaments, the tree. From Wisconsin."

I had been in the house less than 10 minutes and had already made several faux pas. Never for a moment had I suspected Washington had quit producing Christmas trees. Last I'd heard, holiday trees were the fourth largest grossing product of the state.

"Let's head back downstairs. Your brother's probably in the dining room—I'll bet he's still complaining about the new table I bought. It's a Chippendale's."

"Really?" I smiled broadly, thinking we were finally on a subject I knew something about. "I always wondered what those guys did when they weren't dancing."

Her look sent me scurrying down the steps.

In the next hour I learned that wallpaper, placemats and candles *absolutely, positively must* be color coordinated, that patterned China may only be used with patterned crystal if it matches *exactly*, and that a chandelier is considered gauche if it's more than 20 inches above the centerpiece.

As for the dinner itself, I don't remember ever having a feast quite like that one. None of the food even faintly resembled anything I'd ever eaten before. Everyone in my family was raised strictly "Betty Crocker," and here I was being served "The Joy of Cooking."

Turkey a la Champagne, brandied carrots, Grand Marnier ambrosia, and Amaretto cheesecake put my own humble upbringing to shame.

My cousin Louise brought me back to reality. "Can't she cook anything without booze in it?" she hissed, gently patting her pregnant stomach.

"She didn't cook this dinner, she had it catered," I replied, having seen the restaurant wrappings in the kitchen moments before it was all placed on platters.

Nevertheless, the rest of the gathering turned out to be considerably more congenial than usual, and it's a good thing too.

That dinner was the last time my nuclear family all sat down together for a holiday meal. Children and marriages and extended families now pull us in many different directions, and we're each creating new traditions to pass along.

And in my own household, that Amaretto cheesecake is one new tradition I'm happy to embrace!

Male Procrastination

Ok, men, it's December 24th! Get ready... get set... start your credit cards! It's time to begin your Christmas shopping!

Of course women have had their purchases all wrapped and under the tree for weeks, but there seems to be some form of genetic predisposition for men to procrastinate on this particular activity.

As a classic example, I site a certain male figure in the household of my youth. On Christmas Eve, mind you, with less than an hour until every store in our small town closed, he asked me to accompany him to do his Christmas shopping.

Curious, I went along. After walking up and down most of the nearly-empty aisles in the place, he strode confidently to the jewelry counter. "Your birthday's in June, right?" he asked me. I nodded. He picked up three pairs of fake birthstone earrings: June, July and August. Those were the months, respectively, my sister, my mother, and I were born.

"Good." Dad breathed a sigh of relief, "that's done." As we walked to the check-out counter, he added, "Try to look surprised tomorrow morning."

I was surprised all right. Somehow he'd managed to put the wrong tags on his gifts and I ended up with my sister's earrings. But I suppose he gets a little credit for wrapping them himself.

Now I fully admit there are a few stellar exceptions to this stereotype. Those are the guys who don't wait until the last minute. They're the ones who can read a calendar and probably even listen when hints are given about desired gifts.

Those are the men, bless their hearts, who start shopping on December 23.

God Bless Us, Every One

"Christmas is on December 26th this year," said Mom, "at my house."

"Does God know about this?" I asked.

"God doesn't care if we get together at my house."

"I mean about you changing the date of His Son's birthday celebration."

"Your cousin Louise picked it. I let her decide when we'd get together because she has the most relatives to schedule."

"Perfect. With her track record she'll be lucky to get there by the second week of January."

The next week a letter confirmed Mom's invitation. "I forgot to tell you that your friend is invited too," she wrote. "In fact, he might be just the thing to get the rest of the family here; they'll all be curious. Why don't you make up some cute invitations on your computer? Something like, 'Welcome to the family John'."

I picked up the phone. "Mother," I groaned. "It's August. I don't even know if I'll still be seeing John by December, and I don't think it's fair for you to use him as bait. And, I feel I need to point out that I've never heard of a family reunion taking place in a bathroom."

"The bathroom?"

"You left out a comma. Your letter says 'Welcome to the family John. John, like in bathroom, restroom, or head."

Mom made a strange gargling sound. "Must you always critique my letters?"

"I'll take it that's a rhetorical question. So, do you want me to put a toilet on the front of the invitations, or what? 'Welcome to the Family John' might be more appropriate than you think."

"Janet Marie..."

Some things never change. I know I'd better back off and quit pushing Mom's buttons when she uses my middle name.

"All this mother wants for Christmas is for her family to get along." Mom sighed. "Just bring a pie and keep your mouth shut."

"Don't worry," I told her. "I wouldn't dream of missing your party. And I'll ask John if he'd like to come with me."

"Thank you."

In September, Mom called again. "It's about Christmas," she began.

"I'm so sorry to hear it's been canceled," I interrupted hopefully.

She ignored me. "Do you have any extra decorations, or lights, or ornaments or anything I can borrow? I've got a live tree in a redwood tub out on the deck but I don't have anything to decorate it with."

In October Mom started delineating more rules. "No gifts over 10 dollars," she said.

"Ten dollars? *Apiece?* Do I have to spend that much on people I happen to be related to but I don't see for sometimes years on end? How 'bout I just bring a case of smoked salmon, and whoever shows up gets some?"

"Good idea. Your cousin Louise loves smoked

salmon."

"Anyone who shows up *on time* gets salmon; the rest get tuna."

By November Mom began worrying about the weather. "What if it snows and nobody can make it?"

"Then there really is a God."

"Janet Maaa..."

"Chill out, Mom, I said I'd be there."

Just a few days before the big rendezvous I got my final instructions verifying date, time, and number attending.

"Scratch one off the list," she said. "One of your distant relatives joined some kind of cult that doesn't believe in celebrating Christmas."

"Super," I said. "That'll give us someone to talk about."

"Jan," implored Mom, "I'm counting on you to keep the family peace. I want you to set a good example."

"How come I always get the hardest jobs?"

"You're the oldest."

So over the river and through the woods to Mother's house I went—alone. John, I was reminded every time I used the bathroom for several months, was flushed from my life in early October.

On one hand, I didn't want to be the one to spoil Mother's Norman Rockwell idealism. On the other hand, I wasn't sure I could make good on my vow to keep my lips tightly zipped.

Which probably makes our holiday reunion rather typical of those that take place all over America during the holidays. We choose our friends, but we're born with our relatives.

That holiday season, as holiday seasons are meant to inspire, we all made peace in our hearts, resolving to bury the hatchet someplace other than in each other's backs. For good, bad, or indifferent, blood is still thicker than water.

I'm just grateful we didn't get any of that familial blood on Mother's clean carpet.

In Search of the Perfect Christmas Tree

Our procession included four kids all under the age of 12, a small dog, a sharp handsaw and a sharper ax. What in the world was my mother thinking when she sent us off to find 'the perfect Christmas tree'?

In hindsight, now 45, give or take, years later, maybe what she wanted was just a couple hours peace and quiet.

Our little entourage, bundled up against Mother's admonition not to catch cold, dutifully trudged down the railroad tracks from Grampa's farm. Never before had we been trusted to choose the holiday centerpiece for our home! We all tingled with excitement as we set out.

A couple hours later, the adventure had lost a lot of its appeal. Every six to eight foot tree we encountered had a tragic flaw. Most were too sparsely branched. Some had crooked trunks. Others were totally lopsided.

The perfect tree, so plentiful on city tree lots, was apparently as elusive as a white Christmas in Hawaii.

At long last, we decided all the suitable trees easily obtainable along the track had already been harvested by earlier tree-seekers. We'd have to broaden our search— so we turned our eyes upward.

The 50 to 60 foot trees along the track all seemed to have pretty nice-looking tops—much nicer than anything else we'd seen. In desperation, we started sawing and hacking and hoping we could bring one of these mammoth trees down so we could harvest the top seven feet before it got too dark.

Dad found us a couple hours later—exhausted, sweaty, and wishing we'd brought along some water. We were sitting on railway tracks, four little ducks in a row, with our small black dog curled at our feet.

The tree was down, but since none of us had been to lumberjack school, it was only by the grace of some higher power we hadn't entirely blocked the train tracks. But it was close.

Dad quickly cut back the branches that were too close to the rails, and then stood back to survey the top of our conquered monolith. "And you've all decided that is the perfect tree?"

Silently, almost defeated, we all nodded.

"Okay, then," said Dad, "let's get it home."

My little brother started applauding, our dog started barking, and in no time at all, we were on our way back to Grampa's, happily carrying our prize with us.

Mother met us at the driveway. "I'm so glad you're all safe and sound." Then she looked closely at our tree. "Well..."

I'm sure my parents had some kind of adult secret code pass between them.

"Well..." said Mom again, "I was thinking maybe we could put the tree against the wall this year instead of in the front window. And since this tree doesn't have any branches on one side, it will be absolutely perfect against the wall."

There it was. Validation for our "absolutely perfect" tree. It was a great Christmas gift.

Nutcracker Suite

By dinking around on the Internet, I've found some pretty interesting holiday puzzles, games, and rebuses to entertain my friends at parties over the years. Recently, however, I located a really challenging Christmas Song Quiz that nearly drove us all crazy. Here's a sampling:

The red-suited pa is due in this burg
(*Santa Claus is coming to Town*)
Far back in the hay bin
(*Away in the Manger*)
The smogless bewitching hour arrived
(*It Came Upon a Midnight Clear*)
We are Kong, Lear, and Nat Cole
(*We Three Kings*)
Boulder of the tinkling metal spheres
(*Jingle Bell Rock*)

I made up some handouts and passed them out at a holiday gathering. My friends fussed and bartered and traded answers, and they weren't nearly as amused as I was that I had distributed two different puzzle sheets!

In the end, though, a good time was had by all, and 10 friends took home special "prize bags" filled with some pretty cool stuff.

So… What do you call it when two psychiatrists share a penthouse apartment? (*See story title, above!*)

Up on the Housetop

"It's too big," said my then-husband (*whom I'll simply refer to here as Mr. X*), as he survey the tree I'd selected to be our holiday centerpiece.

"I don't care," I replied. "I want a bushy tree to go clear to the ceiling, and all the rest of the trees on this lot are either too short or too sparsely branched."

"I'll give you a good deal on this one," said the young man assisting us. "It's the last big one we're going to have here. We've got another load coming in tomorrow of seven-foot trees and I'd like to have more room for them."

It was our first year in the new place, and I'd invited every friend and relative we had to our holiday open house. I wanted everything to be perfect, and that included having a 12-foot tree go to the ceiling in the high-beamed 12-foot living room.

Dutifully, Mr. X, the eager lot attendant, and a second young man working on the lot loaded the humongous tree into the back of our pickup. It was quiet on the drive home, each of us lost in our own thoughts.

It took both of us, and a whole lot of gumption, to get the tree out of the truck and onto the tarp I spread out on the garage floor, but I kept any whining to myself.

Once inside the garage, Mr. X got out his tape measure. "I told you so," he smirked. "This tree is a little over 15 feet tall. We're going to have to cut about three feet off just to stand it in the living room." He measured three and a half feet from the bottom.

"Wait! Don't cut the bottom off! It's so thick and beautiful! I'd rather have you cut the top off instead."

Mr. X sighed. "It'll be easier to get it in the house if I cut the bottom off."

I'm sure my lower lip stuck out a good two inches as I pouted, tears threatening to roll down my checks. "Please?" I begged through trembling lips.

Mr. X sighed again. "Alright, fine." He took a fresh one-inch slice off the bottom of the trunk so it could soak up more water and walked around to the top with his chain saw in his hand.

"No more than three feet! Promise me!" I winced and closed my eyes. "I can't look!" In a matter of seconds, the top three feet were gone.

Next we tried to put the stand on the bottom of the tree and discovered the trunk was too big around to fit even our heavy-duty, jumbo-sized stand. Mr. X gave me "that look," and without a word, retrieved his machete and started whittling at the trunk.

Finally, with the stand literally hammered into place, we began wrestling the tree through the rec room door. The branches were so wide at the bottom we got it only a short way into the house before we were stuck tight in the doorway.

"I told you so," muttered Mr. X.

He was on the inside, straining, sweating and swearing, and I was on the outside, trying with all my might to press the branches in tighter so he wouldn't strip all the needles off against the doorframe as he yarded the mammoth tree forward.

At long last, we got the tree inside, and turned it around so we could traverse through the dining room and into the living room. I'd already moved all the furniture out of the way, but still we brushed against the chairs on one side and dining room wall on the other.

Mr. X banged his head on the low chandelier and said words I'd never heard before.

Once we dragged the tree into the front room, we plopped down on the couch to catch our breath.

"Gonna need a crane to stand this darn thing up," he said. "Or maybe a pulley."

"We can do it," I assured him. "You just hold the bottom in place and I'll start at the tip and walk the top up, hand over hand."

I got "that look" again.

"Okay," I countered, "I'll hold the base and *you* walk it up."

But lying on the carpet, holding the iron base in place without letting it slide across the floor as Mr. X worked to right the tree turned out to be more than I could manage. We took several runs at it, but still the tree lay on the floor, mocking us.

Finally, Mr. X brought the stepladder inside, along with a 20-foot length of rope, which he looped over the tree about four feet from the top. "Never mind about the stand for now. We'll just go ahead and let it slide against the wall."

"Okay, but..." I didn't like where this was heading.

"You climb up the ladder, and when I get the tree at about a 45 degree angle, you'll be able to grab hold, then I'll go around and pull from the other side with the rope while you push."

Apparently Mr. X had forgotten I don't "do" ladders.

"Just climb halfway up. Just to the third step. It's not that high."

Okay, he'd remembered my thing about heights. So why was he still pointing to the ladder?

"You want this tree up or not?"

I stood there like the proverbial deer in the headlights, unable to move.

"I'll be using the extension ladder propped against the ceiling beam to decorate the top half later; the least you can do is help me stand it up now."

Convincing myself this would be a funny story to tell my friends from my hospital bed, I timidly climbed to the third rung.

"But what if it keeps on going and topples right on over through the plate glass window?"

"Don't even suggest such a thing," said Mr. X.

Thankfully, we got the tree vertical on the first try, the blunted top wedged solidly against the ceiling.

Mr. X took a couple steps back and evaluated the situation. "It's stuck real tight, so you're not going to be able to fuss about where the front is. I'm not turning it."

"No worries," I said, glad to be back on solid ground. "It's perfect right there." I went to the kitchen to get the water pitcher.

"No need to water it," called Mr. X. "There's no room in the stand."

He folded the stepladder and headed back out to the garage while I went to the spare room and began hauling out dozens of boxes of lights and ornaments.

Presently, I heard loud banging and pounding

sounds. Investigating, I stepped out the front door and looked up. There was Mr. X, nailing the top three feet of the tree to the peak of the roof. From the front yard it looked like the tree in the living room extended clear through the top of the house.

"We paid for it, we may as well use it," he called down. "You got any ornaments that are indoor/outdoor?"

I shook my head and laughed. "I'll go get you some garland, but I'm not climbing the ladder to bring it up."

"Deal," he said.

The Reason for the Season

If you took the same history class as I did in college, then you know that the man known as Jesus was not actually born on December 25. He probably wasn't even born during the winter months, as the shepherds were only out with their flocks in the months with milder temperatures.

The date December 25 was mostly likely picked to dissuade solstice rituals and give the masses something else to celebrate at this dark time of the year. A little bait and switch, if you will. Think how closely "the rebirth of the sun" and "the birth of the Son" sound. *Coincidence?* I think not.

Now before you go believing I'm a total heathen here, let me say that I do, indeed, attend Christmas Eve church services every year. And I do, indeed, decorate my house and give gifts and enjoy all the festivities this holiday presents us.

On December 25 Christians everywhere celebrate Christ's mass. And it shouldn't really matter to anyone just *when* He was born, only *that* He was born.

For *Jesus* is the reason for the season.

It's My Party and I'll Sing if I Want To

I have a friend who plays the piano who comes to my Christmas gathering every year with his holiday songbook tucked under his arm. The Piano Man, as I call him, plays for his supper, so to speak, and graciously shares his time and talent.

And every year, he refrains from remarking upon the obviously in need of a tune-up condition of my spinet. I listen in awe as he tinkles the ivories in a manner I'd never imagined could resonate from the instrument residing in *my* rec room.

Boy howdy, can that man play!

Before he finishes the first song, a crowd gathers around him. Tentative at first, the group begins singing along, enthusiasm increasing with each number. And no one apparently notices or pays any attention to the fact that musical talent seemed to have skipped a few of us.

Meaning me.

Of course, that doesn't stop me from singing. I love to sing. I sing all the time. I sing in the shower, I sing in the car, I sing while I'm walking the boardwalk. But rarely do I sing in the company of another human being.

The holidays, however, are special, with special decorations, and special music, and that special, yet fleeting feeling, of peace on earth and goodwill toward all wannabe Christmas carolers. And, after all, it's my house, and my piano, and my party, so who's going to have the nerve to tell me that perhaps I'd make a better listener than a singer?

Certainly no one with his or her mouth full of hors d'ouevres would be so brazen as to suggest to the hostess that the group would sound even better if she practiced the fine art of lip-sync.

So while Andi hits all the right high notes, and Janice harmonizes with all the right low ones, I fill in with volume. Lots and lots of volume. Joyful noise, I call it, and happily sing the first verse of every carol with glee and gusto.

Unfortunately, the second, third, fourth and sometimes fifth verses of these carols are often written in very small print on the bottom of the sheet music. And The Piano Man often has the only copy of the music on the stand in front of him.

Not-to-worry, while T.P.M. plays the introductions and the chords between the verses, I simply step close enough to rest my chin on his shoulder and read ahead. Then I straighten up and rejoin the chorus.

"You don't have to move back," said T.P.M. a couple years ago, "I kind of like being cheek to cheek."

"No way," I replied, stifling the beginnings of a blush. "I'm not going to sing in your ear. Then you'd know beyond a shadow of a doubt that I'm the one who's been standing behind you singing so far off-key."

"That's okay," said my former friend Shelia, "we've been looking for that key for a long time. Thanks for finding it for us."

It's a good thing I have a pretty thick skin. It's also a good thing that looks don't really kill.

We sang a couple dozen more carols before taking

a break. "Do you play anything classical?" asked Suzanne, taking a seat on the couch.

T.P.M. began playing something vaguely familiar to my untrained ear, but I'll never be a winner on "Name That Tune," no matter how many notes I'm given.

The music was indeed lovely; we listened respectfully. Then our house musician began another, livelier piece. "I forget the exact name of this," he said, "but I think it has something to do with butterflies."

A shy, quiet, retiring, usually-subdued, bespectacled fellow over six feet tall whom I'll call Dave, suddenly jumped up from the corner recliner and onto his feet. He took a couple stag leaps across the rec room carpet and did several rather crazily inept pirouettes. "I can't help it!" he exclaimed. "I'm inspired!"

Stephanie's eyes nearly popped out of her head. "Who are you?!" she exclaimed, "and what have you done with my husband?!"

"And you guys thought my *singing* was bad!" I gasped out between guffaws. "Here I was, thoroughly enjoying our down home Christmas Caroling, when the dance of the bearded ballerina steals the spotlight!"

The Piano Man gamely finished the piece he'd begun, then played the very recognizable theme from the Charlie Brown television specials, after which we all sat in companionable silence for a few moments.

Stephanie, still dazed by the floorshow, slowly shook her head. "Madam Butterfly and the Karaoke Christmas Carolers," she said softly. "Now I've seen and heard it all."

Decorating the Courthouse Tree

South Bend is the present-day county seat of Pacific County. The good people of South Bend swiped the county records in a Sunday evening raid on Oysterville, but *this* story is about Christmas decorations.

Across Willapa Bay, South Bend is just a short boat ride away. But by land, it's a full 50 miles to the northeast of the Long Beach peninsula. And sometimes, it feels as though we live on another planet altogether.

One year when I was teaching fourth grade, I had a phone conversation with a friend of mine who worked at the county courthouse. He told me the elementary children of South Bend would be making ornaments for the holiday tree in the courthouse foyer.

"Does anyone up there know our peninsula children are still at part of this county?" I asked, rather annoyed. "How come we're not invited to participate?"

My friend hemmed and hawed, and a few days later he called to find out if my class would like to make some ornaments for the official tree.

"I thought you'd never ask. When do you need them?"

"I'll have to pick them up this weekend," he said. "The tree goes up right after Thanksgiving."

It was Wednesday. Regular art class was on Friday. This was doable.

"How many decorations would you like?"

"It's a huge tree," he said. "Goes all the way up almost to the chandelier in the rotunda. So three or four hundred ought to do it."

"Say what?!"

"Your class will be named in the display in the foyer," he said, "so make the decorations something you'll be proud to have your name on."

Cripes! What had I gotten myself into?

Thankfully, I'd recently seen an art project for Danish heart ornaments that didn't look too difficult in a woman's magazine. Many in our town hail from north Atlantic countries, so I figured it was close enough.

Before school Thursday morning I gathered all the red, green and white construction paper I could find and two skeins of red yarn. Then I surprised my students by proclaiming an all-morning art class.

But these were wiggly nine and 10 year olds, and some of them didn't know the first thing about "weaving" three by six inch pieces of construction paper.

Teachers are taught to constantly "monitor and adjust," so I backed up a step and demonstrated the project with oversized pieces. Then I paired up my students so that everyone had a "mentor" to help them.

We made red and green, red and white, green and white, all red, and all green heart ornaments the entire morning. The students printed their names on one side of each decoration they completed. Some got rather fancy, and added glitter or small foil stars to their creations.

By lunchtime, we had over 200 Danish hearts completed, all tied with bright red yarn and ready to go.

But 200 is not three to four hundred, and after

lunch we were back at it. My students were losing interest in the project, but I encouraged them to forge ahead by bribing them with a promised extra recess.

We hit our target number—350—just before last recess at 2:00, and since it was so nice outside, instead of the regular 10-minute break, I let them play for nearly half an hour, since we'd skipped PE class. While they played, I contemplated what we'd learned today.

Math was used to measure the one-inch strips of paper. Hand-eye coordination was necessary for the weaving. They learned about design as they chose the color combinations. Cooperation was fostered between students as they helped each other.

We'd written a class letter to the people at the courthouse thanking them for including us in their project, so check off English and spelling.

I decided to lump it all under "Community Service" and checked off social studies as well. Turns out the day was a stellar one for integrated learning.

In December, I made a special trip to the South Bend courthouse to see the fruits of our labor in action. The tree was magnificent, decked out in small lights as well as our 350 Danish Hearts. I wondered who'd tied them all on as I walked around the tree, smiling at the names of my students printed on their creations.

Climbing to the second floor, I took pictures of the tree from many angles to share with my class. I was sure that few of them would make the trip to South Bend just to see the decorated tree.

It is, after all, like traveling to another planet.

A Christmas Cantata

I've been thinking of making my mark in the literary world with a twenty-first century feminist remake of the old standard Dicken's tale. I haven't quite got all the bugs worked out of the script yet, but it goes something like this:

SCENE ONE: Eleanor Scroojé, CEO of Scroojé Enterprises, an elite nation-wide escort service headquartered in Houston and promoting Southern Comfort Hospitality, is informing one of her employees that she may certainly *NOT* quit early on Christmas Eve...

"But Boss," says perky blue-eyed Bobbi Cratchit, "I'm a single mom with three kids all waiting for up for Santa tonight. Can't one of the other gals watch Mr. Bumstead dance on the table with a lampshade on his head during his annual company Christmas party?"

"Save your sob story," says Eleanor, "Mr. B. specifically requested you, and you know he's one of our most influential clients. He also tips well. Very well. So if you want to keep your job, you'll spend your evening hanging on his arm, as well as his every word, and laughing at all his ribald jokes."

SCENE TWO: Eleanor is propped up on a myriad of satin pillows in a cranberry silk comforter-covered four-poster bed reading a Stephen King novel when she nods off. She dreams of Christmas Past, where a rather plain, homely girl of 17 begs her poor mother for money to go to charm school to learn the fine art of etiquette and the social graces necessary to rise above her impoverished beginnings...

"Please, Mom!" Elly whines. "Don't you want me to make something of myself? All my friends are enrolling in the Evelyn Wood Finishing School next semester. If I don't go to school there I'll never be on the cover of 'Mademoiselle'."

"If I give you the tuition for that school," says her doting mother, "there won't be any money left for your seven brothers' Christmas gifts this year."

"Mom, you're the greatest!" Elly heartily embraces her mother and spins her around on the threadbare living room carpet.

SCENE THREE: Eleanor awakens and looks at a picture of her mother on the nightstand next to her bed.

"See Mom? I *am* somebody. You'd be proud of me, Mom. I've got my own business now. I've got *money*."

Her mother's picture speaks to her: "Elly girl, does all your money make you happy? How can I be proud of someone who honors the accumulation of wealth above the spirit of Christmas?" Eleanor shakes her head and blinks her eyes.

"Do you want to see what will become of you if you don't change your selfish ways?" her mother continues. "Turn on your big-screen TV, Honey... Take a good look at your future."

Eleanor shakily picks up the remote and hesitantly clicks it. She sees herself as a lonely old spinster sitting in a cocktail bar wearing an exorbitant amount of blue eye-shadow and slurping down vodka martinis. "I'm shomebody," slurs the elderly Eleanor to the man seated next to her. The man looks her up and down, then picks up his drink and moves a few barstools away. "Hey," calls Eleanor, "I'm shomebody!"

The present day Eleanor turns off the TV and cowers in her bed, pulling the covers up over her head.

SCENE FOUR: It is morning. Eleanor gets out of bed in her brocade pajamas and quickly pulls open the window. "Boy!" she calls out to a child in the street. "Boy! What day is it?"

"December 26th," replies the voice outside the window. "The day after Christmas."

"Thank goodness!" says Eleanor Scroojé. "I've slept through Christmas! It's another workday! Another chance for my girls to make me more money!" And she happily hums "Zippity-do-dah" as she exits the room.

*   *   *   *   *

Like I said, I haven't got it quite ready for production yet. I might throw in a few lines for Bobbi's youngest daughter, Tiny Tina, who wants a real live daddy, not just a Sugar Daddy, for Christmas. Or maybe I'll have Bobbi get fired for going home early to read "A Visit from St. Nicholas" in a soft southern drawl to her kids before tucking them in to dream their visions of dancing sugar plums.

But however it plays out, I know one thing for certain: Eleanor will swear off reading Stephen King novels for the rest of her life.

What else would have given her such bizarre nightmares?

The Wisest of Wise Men

Third grader Danny was hard at work coloring a picture to illustrate an alphabetical Christmas poem my class had worked so hard to memorize. As he studiously colored, his tongue was clearly visible, clenched between his teeth. His concentration was amazing, considering how active and fidgety he usually was.

Completing a portion of his picture, Danny raised his head to take a short break. He exhaled loudly, rotated his shoulders, and looked over at a neighboring student's artwork. He scowled.

"Hey! Just whaddya think you're doin'?" he asked his classmate. He got up out of his seat and quizzically scrutinized his neighbor's drawing, placing his hands on his hips and tilting his head, squinting at it.

"K is for Kings, you'll recall there were three," recited his friend in a singsong manner, not bothering to look up from his work.

"Yeah," said Danny, "I see the three people, but your picture's all wrong."

"It is not!" The boy pulled his paper closer to him in a slightly defensive manner.

"Yes it is!" shouted a belligerent Danny. "You've got the kings wearing pants!" He stomped his foot for emphasis.

"So?"

"So these three kings wore robes! Long, heavy robes

made of fur and stuff like that, and you've got them all dressed up in *designer jeans!*"

Not to be deterred, the child continued blissfully coloring. "I thought it would be okay to make it a little more modern," he whispered, more to himself than anyone else. Then he straightened up and looked Danny in the eye. "And since it's *my* picture, that's the way it's going to be. I'm the artist, and I say so."

Danny stood his ground and chewed on his lower lip. He leaned first on one foot and then the other, considering. Finally, he shrugged and said, "That's an artist for you," and returned to his seat to work on his own picture.

Crisis averted, and the three kings arrived sporting an updated wardrobe.

A Magical, Musical Christmas

Marlene flipped through the yellow pages, vocalizing her dismay to her neighbor and best friend Shelly, as she did so. "There's no listing for music, musical instruments, musicians, pianos, piano tuners, or tuners of any kind... Oh, the joy of living in a small town!" She shook her head. "Got any suggestions?" She handed Shelly the phone book.

"As a matter of fact," said Shelly, setting down her coffee mug and accepting the proffered book, "I do."

Marlene raised an eyebrow. "Ok, Mrs. Smarty-pants, just where are you going to find a professional piano tuner for me?"

"I'll call the church," said Shelly matter-of-factly. "Somebody must tune all *their* pianos. Between the sanctuary, the fellowship room, and the choir room, they've got three of them."

A sigh of relief escaped Marlene. She smiled at Shelly. "How long were you going to let me stew before you offered this choice bit of information?"

Shelly smiled back. "Not too much longer. Since your Christmas party isn't for another two weeks, I still had a few days grace before I came to the rescue."

Shelly placed a call to the church office, got the needed information, and wrote the number down. "Here you go," she said, pushing the notepad in front of Marlene. "Think you can take it from here?"

Shelly stood to leave, gave her friend a hug and said, "Try not to stress so much, it's not good for you." She ducked out the door before Marlene could reply.

"You're in luck," said the elderly-sounding male voice on the other end of the line. "This is my busiest time of the year, but I think I can squeeze you in next Thursday at 4:30. Will that be okay?"

Marlene thought quickly. "Yes," she said, "that will be fine. I won't be home until 5:30 myself, but I have a neighbor who can let you in."

Thursday evening, Marlene hustled through her own front door and came to an abrupt halt. She heard a strange yet wonderful combination of music, singing, and laughter coming from her living room. She shrugged out of her coat and went straight to the source of the merriment.

Shelly was standing next to the piano, holding a child's book of popular Christmas tunes open so that she and a young curly-haired boy Marlene didn't recognize could both see the words. In a nearby rocking chair sat another unfamiliar man about Marlene's age, rocking and singing along without looking at the book. An older man stroked the piano keys with gusto and was encouraging them to sing another verse.

"Well," said Marlene, making her presence known, "this certainly looks like a Norman Rockwell moment!" She smiled tentatively, and asked Shelly, "Who are all these people, and what are they doing in my house?"

Shelly laughed. She put her hand on the senior gentleman's shoulder. "This is Mr. Santano, the best piano tuner in at least three counties." She pointed to the man in the rocking chair. "And this is Mr. Santano, his son." She turned the boy to face Marlene. "And this handsome young fellow is Mr. Santano, the son of the son."

"Pleased to meet you," said the Santanos in unison, nodding their heads.

"And it took all of you to tune my piano?" asked Marlene.

"It's a family affair," said the Santano in the rocking chair. He had the same curly hair as the boy, and a warm and genuine smile like his father. "Dad doesn't drive any more, and my son comes along so we don't need to hire a babysitter."

"I'm too old for a babysitter," protested the young man. "I come along to help Grandpa do the tune-ups."

"And he's a pretty good little assistant, too," chimed in the elder Santano. He extended his hand to Marlene. "My name's Jim," he said.

"And I'm James," said his son.

"Let me guess," said Marlene, bending down to look the youngest Santano in the eye. "Is your name Jimmy?"

"Heck, no," he replied. "My name's Eddie." Then he grinned. "Short for James Edward Santano the Third."

Marlene smiled. "It's nice to meet all three of you," she said, making brief eye contact with each of them.

James stood up and cleared his throat. "I believe," he said, looking at his watch, "that we're through here, and it's Eddie's turn to make dinner."

Marlene turned to Shelly with an inquiring look.

"These three guys are all bachelors," said Shelly, "so they rotate the cooking responsibilities."

"And tonight it's macaroni and cheese!" said Eddie

excitedly. "I make it all by myself, too!" He fairly bounced with anticipation. "Dad taught me how to follow the directions on the box and now I'm a gourmet cook!" He gave Marlene another big grin and lowered his voice. "Only I can't remember what 'gourmet' means."

Marlene laughed. "It means 'very good,' and I just bet you are."

James touched his son's shoulder. "Time to help Grandpa pack up his tools."

While Eddie did as he was told, Marlene said good-bye to Shelly, who needed to get home to fix dinner for her own family.

"And what are your plans for dinner tonight?" asked James. "I'll bet Eddie wouldn't mind making a double batch of his famous mac 'n cheese." His deep brown eyes implied much more than a simple dinner invitation.

"Say yes!" said Eddie, hopping up and down again.

"Well," said Marlene, surveying the smiling trio, "I'll say 'yes' on one condition." She hesitated while the three of them looked at her expectantly. "You must promise me you'll all come to my Christmas party next weekend and help us sing carols."

"It's a deal!" said Eddie, without waiting for his father to respond.

"It's the best deal I've heard in a long time," said James, smiling happily.

Jim snapped his toolbox closed and headed toward the door whistling, "It's beginning to look a lot like Christmas…"

Upside-down Christmas Tree

"You did what?" I asked my friend Anna Marie, certain that the static on our phone connection had garbled the message.

"I hung the Christmas tree from the ceiling," she repeated.

"Oh... Ok... I've also tied mine to the ceiling to keep it from tipping over many times. I use fishing line."

"No," said Anna Marie, "I mean we hung it *upside down* from the ceiling."

"Upside-down?"

"Is there an echo in here?" Anna Marie laughed. "You don't have to repeat everything I say."

"I'm just trying to wrap my mind around the concept," I replied.

"It's really a no-brainer," said Anna Marie. "We have no room to put up a standard Christmas tree, so we had to improvise."

"That's improvising, all right. Tell me more."

"There's more space to put presents underneath it, the dog can't knock it over, and the star on the top is now more of a centrally-located focal point for the kids."

"What about tinsel?" I asked. "Doesn't it look ridiculous hanging down like fringe on a lampshade?"

"Tinsel is politically, or at least environmentally, incorrect."

"Hey there! Be careful what you say. I always

remove every single strand of tinsel and dispose of it properly before taking out the tree."

"Then you're the exception," said Anna Marie. "But let's get back to my reasons for the inverted tree."

"Yes, let's," I agreed.

"You know all those especially pretty ornaments you have?"

"Yeah?"

"Well, often they get hidden in the branches of a standard tree. On mine, they're clearly visible."

"Okay, go on."

"And here's another good reason to do it this way," she began. "You can walk all around the tree and see it from every angle; it's not shoved up against a window or wall."

"So how do you water it?"

"It's not up long enough to worry about that," said Anna Marie. "As soon as it starts showing signs of drying out, it's time to take it down."

"Hhmm... Well, for your house, and for a standard 7-foot tree, I'll concede it's an... uh... interesting idea," I finally conceded. "But it would never work here."

"And why not? Do you fear change?"

"No, I just fear that suggesting we suspend a 12-foot tree by its base to the 12-foot ceiling would leave me without much hope of having any friends left by Christmas."

"You're right," Anna Marie agreed, laughing. "It's not for everybody."

The Governor's Christmas Card

Over two decades ago, with a heart full of seasonal joy and jubilation, I mailed out my annual, and very creative, Christmas cards. I've always taken pride in designing uniquely homemade (*some may say bizarre, or at the very least, unusual*) greetings, and that year stands out as one of the best.

On the front of the card was an authentic, non-retouched photo of me, arm-in-arm with newly-elected Governor Lowry. We're both smiling broadly. Inside the card, in my very own green felt-tipped script, the greeting read: "The Governor and I wish you the very merriest Christmas ever."

Never mind how, or when, I came by the picture. Just trust me when I say that there was absolutely no trick photography involved, no blackmail, and that the picture was taken with both our consents.

The Christmas card idea was the brainchild of a dyed-in-the-wool Democrat; I simply could not pass up such a golden opportunity in a victorious election year. I took particular pleasure in mailing a few of these cards out to my Republican friends. (*Yes, for the first time, I'm publicly admitting to having a couple of those...*)

The responses were varied. Many of my Democrat card-receivers hooted with delight:

"You never cease to crack me up, Jan."

"Atta girl!"

"I wish I'd thought of doing that!"

Other responses, and you can guess from which political party, were not so enthusiastic:

"One of these days, JB, you're gonna get your butt arrested for fraud."

(*I hastily checked into this possibility. Apparently an elected official is public domain, and since I wasn't using his image to promote a cause or sell a product, I'm in the clear. Besides, I genuinely believe Governor Lowry would be more than happy to wish my friends a Merry Christmas; for the most part, they are really very nice people, voting records notwithstanding.*)

"Who was that elderly gentleman in the picture with you?" wrote one rather snide friend. "Is he British? Is that why you call him *Governor*?"

"Let's wait and see what you have to say about good old Mike *next year*," said another.

Well, it's hard to believe, but when next year arrived, I was still a staunch supporter of the Gov. I could readily identify with the trials and tribulations he faced after being elected. All too vividly I remembered way back when I was the 'M' word (*married*) and stared my first budget shortfall square in the face one January. Like Governor Lowry, it was an unexpected debt that I inherited. Like Governor Lowry, I vowed never to be blindsided like that again. I wasn't, and he... well, let's get back to the subject at hand.

The following November I got out my Christmas card list and discovered one of previous year's greetings stashed among the stickers and seals. On a fluke, I mailed it to the Governor, explaining my holiday prank. I'd heard he had a great sense of humor, and I thought he might get a kick out of it.

But as soon as the card left my possession at the post office, I began to worry. What if he *didn't* think it was funny?

The days passed into weeks, and I thought I may have been expecting too much to assume that my innocuous little greeting card would actually make it into the same hands that ran our state. By the 21st of December, I didn't know if I should breathe a sigh of relief that no offense was taken, or be miffed because I got no response. I supposed it *was* asking a bit much for him to answer my holiday greeting, even if it did have his very own picture on it. After all, he was a very busy man.

But then, suddenly, there it was: an envelope arrived with the Gov's return address in Olympia! I gingerly opened it, hoping against hope.

The card was generic, just a family photo and rather blandly imprinted with only his name. The kind you can order by the thousands. It held no special message, no handwritten acknowledgment—nothing. I'd simply received a standard return card, as in "I sent you mine, now you send me yours." I wasn't so special after all. I was merely a single constituent, representing only one vote.

Governor Lowry didn't run for a second term. He probably knew some of us weren't quite feeling the love by then. Christmas love not withstanding.

Christmas Angels

Sometimes we don't immediately recognize them—those low-keyed saints who come marching through our lives. But one recent holiday season I made a conscious effort to be more mindful of the myriad of people who help make my own bumpy life function just a little bit smoother.

Take the guy with the truck who got my Christmas tree home from the nursery. I don't have a truck, and it was unlikely the nine-foot tree could be successfully lashed to the top of my car for a safe trip home.

And there's the woman who said she "wanted to feel a part of it," and slipped me some money to help cover the expenses of a big, wonderful holiday gathering.

Another woman braved my perfectionism and came over to help decorate the house, not once, but twice, while I bustled about in my usual December panic mode, wondering if everything would all get done "on schedule."

Then there's the guy who braved it all—The man who "climbed the ladder" and decorated the "top two quadrants" of the tree. Talk about unbridled courage! While I handed up the lights and balls and yes, even tinsel *(God help him)*, this man calmly followed my specific and rather anal-retentive instructions to the letter—and today we're still speaking!

So I want to thank these friends, and many others,

for putting up with a hot-flashing, menopausal, prednisone-taking, somewhat irritable holiday lunatic. Thank you all for coming to my rescue even when I didn't particularly deserve it.

You are my Christmas angels, and I couldn't/wouldn't have done it without you.

Tinseling in the Nude

"You've heard the old saying, 'It's like pulling hen's teeth'?" I asked my dear friend Anna Marie.

"Uh-huh."

"Well, finding help to set up the Christmas tree makes pulling hen's teeth seem like child's play."

"Quit whining," she said. "Just throw a party and invite all your tall, non-acrophobic friends to come over and celebrate 'the trimming of the tree'. Either that, or make up you mind, once and for all, that a six-foot tree is every bit as nice as one that reaches clear to your 12-foot ceiling."

"No way." I shook my head. "That yearly 12-foot tree is a symbol of my independence. When I got divorced, I swore I wouldn't scale down just because I didn't have a live-in tree-trimmer. It's a matter of personal pride and principle."

"Principles or not," said Anna Marie, "I'll help you with the ornaments, but that's it."

"Terrific!" I beamed. "I've got the crew in place to bring it into the house and set it up, another contingent to man the ladders and get the lights on it, and you'll nicely round out the baubles and balls brigade."

The only thing left was tinsel. What is it about tinsel anyway? Even the mention of the word sends grown men and women screaming for asylum.

"Wait!" I implored the hordes of so-called friends

abandoning my living room. "Think of it as a 'growing experience.' After tonight you can tell everyone you have looked tinseling square in the eye and come away unscathed!"

"I promised my sitter I'd be home by nine."

"I came over here right after dinner, and I'm sure the dishes are through soaking by now."

"My laundry is piled three feet higher than the washer."

"I've been neglecting my cat. I promised tonight I'd spend some quality time with him tonight."

"Face it Jan," said Anna Marie, the last rat to leave, "it's not that we don't love you, we just don't *do* tinsel."

So now I had a decision to make. Could I live with a non-tinseled tree, or would I have to manage to put it all on by myself? I decided to sleep on it.

Everything looked rosier first thing in the morning—a clear, crisp, December day. I pulled on my bathrobe and opened the drapes to survey the behemoth dominating my living quarters. What a glorious tree! But yes, I determined, it needed tinsel.

I fixed a cup of cocoa, turned on the stereo, and opened the first of 24 packages of icicles. A 12-foot tree takes 24 packages; it's in the rule book.

Several hours later, and about two-thirds finished, I realized that static cling was causing my clothing to take off about as much tinsel as I put on with each trip around the tree. I looked like a giant foil orb.

No problem. I had only a few more turns around the fir to complete the job. I set my glasses on the coffee table and shucked off my robe and nightgown. I live in the woods; I was not expecting company.

Singing along with Mitch Miller and his band, I worked my way once again around the back of the tree. The *back* of the tree, of course, is against the *front* windows.

Suddenly, my peripheral vision caught a movement out in the driveway. Something far bigger than my cat was out there, and here I was, caught buck-naked tinseling to the tune of "Silent Night."

I dropped to the floor. I hadn't seen a car pull in, but perhaps someone had walked into the yard from the road. My robe, draped across a dining room chair, was miles away. I couldn't even get to my glasses without risking further exposure.

Gathering courage, I raised up to peer, like Kilroy, over the edge of the windowsill. At the same time, whatever it was out there also raised up to get a better look.

And there we were, nose-to-nose, with only the plate glass window separating us: bare on the inside, and *bear* on the outside.

I don't know which of us was more startled. But I do know which one of us quickly got to her feet, retrieved her glasses and bathrobe and watched a very large, very confused bear lumber off into the woods.

I'll never know what possessed that bear to rouse itself from a time of supposed hibernation to pay me an early morning visit. The only thing I know for sure is that this is one woman who is never, ever, going to be caught tinseling in the nude again by neither man nor beast!

The Wench Who Stole Christmas

"Auntie," said my darling niece one rainy Saturday afternoon while rummaging through my closet, "let's play dress-up."

Little did my darling niece know, but her auntie plays dress-up all the time. That's why I have boxes and drawers full of outlandish clothes for almost every occasion. Give me the slightest reason to pull on a costume, and I'm there.

Something mysterious and relatively anonymous happens when I put on a costume. It's not really me behaving this way, it's the character I'm playing. "Dressing up" gives me license to act out in a way that otherwise might be deemed a tad bit eccentric, and that's at the very least.

The older I get, the more I appreciate the word eccentric.

During my teaching career, I dressed up for my work as a seventh grade social studies teacher disguised as the wizard Merlin, Joan of Arc, and a medieval scullery maid. Homecoming week I wore an authentic 60s tie-dyed t-shirt, faded jeans, headband, peace-sign earrings and beaded vest. I know for sure the outfit was "authentic" because I originally wore it in the 1960s.

Naturally, I donned cowgirl garb for a back-to-school barbecue and Hoe Down, and I fit right in with Lil' Abner and the other Dogpatch residents during a

Sadie Hawkins Day Dance.

And then there's Halloween! A truly inspired holiday destined to be the delight of any self-respecting wannabe actor!

Yet my finest fantasy hour (*thus far*) came not on Halloween, but during a Christmas party. The gala event happened to land on the anniversary of the Boston Tea Party, practically *mandating* a Colonial Christmas theme.

Secondhand shops are the godsend of costume creators. By scouring the local thrift stores, I found a wonderful burgundy bed skirt from which to make a multi-ruffled colonial-style skirt. Cutting the bottom off a gauzy white blouse, there was enough "extra" material to add wide bell sleeves.

A sheer curtain valance was just the ticket to make a realistic-looking bonnet for the costume. A tight woolen vest of burgundy and forest green finished off the outfit. After sewing eyelet lace around the hem of the skirt and blouse sleeves, and adding black stockings and low-heeled shoes, the ensemble was complete.

The serving wench, a.k.a. "The Wench Who Stole Christmas," was an unbridled success. It may not have been quite as classy as the duds George or Martha Washington paraded around in, or as unique as the elk hide draped, antler-wearing, face-painted Native American celebrating the reason behind the Boston Tea Party, but it was, nevertheless, a pretty cool costume.

And once I have a costume on, there's no stopping me. Sometimes it doesn't even take a full-bodied outfit. At the high school audience-participation play, "Southern Fried Murder," an affectatious accent inspired me to become a whole 'nother persona.

Just slipping on a pair of red high-heels can transport me into an entirely different dimension.

Sylvia, the psychic from Seattle, was born when I put on a pair red shoes. Now whenever I'm wearing them, I slip easily into a mode tailor-made to tell fortunes, predict horoscopes, and read knees. Yes, knees—but I'll save *that* story for another time.

Truth be told, I've never truly enjoyed being an "adult." What's *that* supposed to mean? Do I have put my childish games aside? Am I "too mature" to sing silly songs and make bunnies out of pancake batter? Do I have to be stern and respectable and (*gulp!*) responsible? Heaven forbid! That goes against my belief that life wasn't *meant* to be taken quite so seriously.

There are many books and tapes explaining how to "get in touch with your inner child." And they all tell us our inner children are screaming for us to lighten up. No surprise there. I'm sure ulcers are the result of a stifled inner child. Adults would be wise to embrace joys of letting go of and having some fun.

Fortunately, we have darling young nieces and nephews and children and grandchildren to help us keep a healthy perspective.

There are many far-reaching benefits of "playing pretend," but you'll have to experience them for yourself. This holiday season I challenge each of you to get all dressed up and then let your hair down.

You can start small. Wear an elf hat or reindeer antlers while you Christmas shop. Risk being called "foolish." Come on out and play!

Be Careful What You Wish For

My friend Idaho Steve had sent me a plain manila envelope a few days before Christmas one year with these instructions written boldly across the back: "Put this under your tree! Do not open until Christmas! Trust me! I will know if you open it earlier!"

Now in my heart of hearts, I knew Steve wouldn't *really* know if I peeked before Christmas, but as a matter of personal pride, I wanted to be able to tell him truthfully say I had adhered to his mandate.

Christmas morning I checked to see that my cat Bubba hadn't left any more snacks for later under the tree, and then began unwrapping my gifts. I saved Steve's for last, and it's a good thing, too. After I saw what he'd sent me, I shrieked and began laughing so hysterically that poor Bubba ran for cover. Steve was right; if I had opened the envelope any sooner than Christmas Day, he *would* have known about it, because I would have *immediately* called him!

Steve had taken a full-length picture of himself, fresh out of the shower, in the bathroom mirror. The flash from the camera "haloed" his head, so his face was totally unrecognizable. On the back of the photo he'd written: "You told me you wanted to find a naked man under your tree on Christmas morning, and I care enough to send the very best. Love, Steve."

God blesses those with a twisted sense of humor.

A Letter to Santa

Dear Santa,

How are you? I am fine. How is Mrs. Claus? And the elves? Please give the reindeer an extra carrot for me—we're all counting on them Christmas Eve!

I have been a very good girl this year. Very, very, very good. So good I've been almost boring, but at least I know it keeps me from getting coal in my stocking.

Most everything I want I already have. My mother says I am entirely too spoiled and that I shouldn't bother you by writing this year. But this year I'm not writing just for me. This year I'm asking for you to bring something for a few little friends of mine.

You see, Santa, I'm worried about some of my fourth graders. So many of them don't believe in you. So many of them have stopped believing in magic altogether. It must be very sad for them, and even sadder for you. I can't begin to imagine what the world would be like if no one believed in hope, or love, or miracles.

Sometimes a child will quietly approach me and ask if I *personally* believe in Santa Claus. Being a teacher, a sacred trust is put on the line. Rest assured, Santa, I'll never let you down—I *always* tell them the absolute truth.

I tell them about the time I discovered the sleigh tracks in the backyard and counted 36 hoof prints in the snow. (*'Thirty-six!' they exclaim, "but four hooves times eight reindeer is 32!" "Don't forget Rudolph," I say, not missing the opportunity for an object lesson in multiplication.*)

I tell them about the time two of your elves knocked on my front door on December 23 and asked how late my family would be enjoying a fire in the fireplace the next evening. "We're members of Santa's Safety Committee," they explained. "Santa's suit is made of fire-retardant material, but he doesn't want to take any chances. Besides, we don't mind taking the time off to do this survey—it's a nice break from building toys all day!"

I tell them about the time I pulled on your beard when I was having my picture taken with you, and how I found nothing but ashes in my stocking on Christmas morning. Don't worry Santa, Mom made me clean the whole mess up before I could open *any* of my other presents. (*By the way, thanks for not holding a grudge—I really enjoyed the new skis the following year!*)

And finally, Santa, I tell my children about all the years I've waited up, watched the sky, and tried to pick out the twinkling lights that meant your sleigh was nearing my house. I still do that, you know, but instead of falling asleep at the window and waking up with a crick in my neck, I crawl into bed and listen to Christmas music when I start getting too sleepy.

So what do I want for my little friends? It's the biggest gift I've ever asked for, but I don't know where else to turn. And even though it's asking a lot, I'm sure you'll find plenty of room for it in your sleigh.

Santa, dearest Santa, a great many of my children are in desperate need of an extra-large helping of

Christmas Magic. They need hugs and smiles and pats on the back just for being who they are.

My kids need moms and dads and grandparents who will spend time with them sharing the joys of the holidays. They need family traditions like baking cookies and sending cards and caroling at the nursing homes. They need secret shopping trips and someone to take them to Sunday School to learn the *real* reason behind the season.

I realize this is a rather large request. Gigantic. Mammoth. Enormous. Colossal. But Christmas Spirit is not something we can legislate or order at the drive-thru window. It takes a commitment of *time* and it's kind of tough to wrap. But it's worth it, Santa, you know it is. Our children are only children for a short time; they deserve our best.

So thank you, Santa, I know in my heart you'll do what you can.

Oh, and Santa, just one more thing: If there's space in your sack to tuck in a little something for me, could you please bring me a ticket to Italy? Like I said, I've been a very, very, *VERY* good girl...

Love and Kisses,
Jannie B.

The Noel House

What a joy it is in the dark of December to see all the homes lit up with Christmas lights.

One particular house I used to pass each night always cheered me at the end of a long workday. No matter what, that light display never failed to comfort me and give me a feeling of absolute hope.

It was a large house with a big double garage set back a little from the road, commanding attention as if it were on stage. There were multi-colored lights strung along every eave and beam, framing each window and outlining the doors and walkways. In the front yard were several large animated deer made of small white lights.

But the focal point was clearly the roof. There, in letters at least 10 feet high and four feet wide, the word "NOEL" was lit up like... well, like a good little kid's face on Christmas morning!

I dubbed it "The Noel House," and for over a decade, I looked forward to the weekend after Thanksgiving, when the shining lights at night would tell me I was almost home. Many times I pulled over to the side of the road for just a moment, to say a quick prayer, take a deep breath, and get myself re-centered.

Then one year, all was dark. Oh how I wanted to go knock on the door and ask if everyone was all right! Later I learned there *had* been a serious illness in the family, and there'd been no time to put up any Christmas decorations that year.

Today, new owners live in The Noel House, and they tried, but it's just not the same. Their chainmail gates are always closed, and the "NOEL" sign now sits by itself on the lower garage roof, all in green bulbs, and not easily seen from the roadway.

I wish I'd ever thought to stop and take a picture when The Noel House was fully decorated. Maybe the new owners just don't realize what an institution it was. Or maybe they have other priorities in December— priorities that don't include house lighting.

This loss saddens me, and I find myself going out of my way to either arrive back home in daylight, or drive another route home.

"The first Noel, the angels did say, was to certain poor shepherds in fields as they lay..."

I close my eyes and image The Noel House all lit up again. Some things are far too dear not to remember exactly the way they were.

Inside-out Carolers

One Christmas I was asked to share some of my holiday stories with the Bayside Singers, a local volunteer choir right here on the Long Beach Peninsula in southwest Washington state.

They matched my stories, and those of others, to seasonal song selections and twice on the first Sunday of December, we all performed in the holiday show.

Afterward, one of the singers invited everyone back to her house for lasagna, salad, and garlic bread. It was a festive occasion, everyone dressed in their "Sunday best," but with much laughing and camaraderie, and I was thrilled to be a part of it.

December's a happily bustling time of year, and I had too much left to do before the big day, so I was among the first to thank the hostess and head for my car.

Outside the house, I could see many silhouettes of those still inside as they gathered around the spinet piano, still eager to lift their voices in song. The strains of familiar carols wrapped around me and I stood stock-still, enjoying the Norman Rockwell moment. But how could he have managed to paint the softly sentimental and purely nostalgic sounds wafting through the night?

My to-do list would wait just a little longer.

For Men Only

Women already know what women want for Christmas. We're not really all that complicated if a guy is willing to just sit up and pay attention.

It's not that we women are particularly shy about conveying our wishes—I believe it's just that men often are very poor receptors for this type of information. Oh, they hear us alright, but they just don't listen very well.

No matter how many hints we give them.

Newly-formed couples have an especially difficult time with this. Take Karen and Bart for example. Karen and Bart had been going together for many months when December rolled around one year. At the mall, they window-shopped every boutique, hand-in-hand.

"Oh," breathed Karen as they passed the jewelry store. "Isn't that gorgeous?" She pointed to a large diamond engagement ring.

"Uh-huh," said Bart. "Very sparkly." He didn't seem to be pushing her on to the next window in any hurry, so Karen figured the message had been received.

On Christmas morning Bart and Karen opened their presents separately, each at their parents' home.

Karen received a clock from Bart. Granted, the clock matched the decor in her bedroom, but surely there must be more to this first Christmas gift. She opened the battery compartment and removed the batteries. She shook it. She got out a screwdriver and disassembled the entire timepiece. *No ring!*

Fortunately, her teenage son was able to reassemble the clock before Bart arrived that evening for dinner.

Poor Karen! But even those women who've been married for a few years seem to be on the failing end of the annual gift exchange more often than not. A recent survey of women married between two and 20 years revealed this list of commonly received gifts from their husbands: various small appliances, trash compactors, garage door openers, lawn mowers, recliners, living room lamps, food processors and stainless steel mixing bowls.

My personal favorite is the woman who received a purebred golden retriever for Christmas—allegedly to guard the house when her husband wasn't out duck hunting.

As a teenager, I once had the opportunity to Christmas shop with my father. After over two hours of deliberation, carefully making my selections and feeling rather proud of myself for being so creative and organized, I encountered my father on the way to the checkout.

He stood frowning, hands in pockets, rocking back and forth agitatedly on the heels of his shoes. I thought his apparent impatience must be aimed at me—surely his own purchases were already paid for and stored in the trunk of the car.

"Say," he began tentatively, "your birthday is in June, right?"

"Yes."

"Good. I remembered your sister's and mother's birthday months, but I wasn't sure about yours." With that remark, he brightened, walked directly to the $2.99

earring display, and picked out imitation birthstone earrings for June, July, and August. "There. That's done." He smiled as we both headed toward the check stand. "Your mother's always hinting that she never gets any jewelry. Sorry you have to know what your present is ahead of time. Don't tell the others."

I swear he actually said that. No ceremony, no secret gift-wrapping sessions, no hiding credit card receipts. I dunno... Maybe it's another one of those guy things.

So what *do* women want for Christmas? (*Time to take notes, guys!*)

Women want something personal. Something that took time to think about, something not particularly practical, and something they definitely would not buy for themselves.

Start the list with frilly lace, precious metals, exotic gems, provocative scents, and airline tickets to any place warm. After that, a simple candlelight dinner for two, a new satin robe, and a bottle of bubble bath would certainly be welcome.

Most women I know start dropping hints in mid-October. One year I cleared a space on the refrigerator and put up a picture of a heart-shaped birthstone ring with a little diamond on each side of it. When the guy I was seeing finally noticed the ad, in late November, he casually said, "What's this?"

"Since you asked, I've always wanted a pretty birthstone ring, and those are on sale through the end of this year."

He squinted at the photo. "That's a good price," he agreed.

But that's not what was under the tree for me that year. Instead, I got an office chair, which I love, and really did want, but seriously, did he really think the way deeper into my heart was through office furniture for Christmas?

So pay attention men, if any of you have read this far. A gift certificate to a beauty salon is a thousand times better than a vacuum cleaner.

And women—since some of you are undoubtedly also reading along—you can thank me later!

Bless you, Santa!

Little Jannie was eight and a half when she asked Santa for a blackboard for Christmas. It wasn't on his standard good little girl wish list, but it was what Little Jannie wanted.

"You sure you wouldn't like a nice doll with lots of extra clothes? You could play dress-up with all your other little girlfriends," suggested Santa.

Adamantly, Little Jannie shook her head. "Nope. No dolls, Santa. I want to play teacher, and I need a blackboard."

"Okay," said Santa with a shrug, "I can't argue with that. One blackboard coming right up for one of our future teachers!"

Eagerly, Little Jannie entered the living room on Christmas morning. True to his word, Santa had brought her a blackboard, eraser, and two boxes of chalk—one white, and one of different pastel colors.

"Thanks for the milk and cookies!" said the message scrawled across the chalkboard. It was signed "Love, Santa."

At first Little Jannie didn't want to erase the message. Not everyone had a sample of Santa's handwriting, and this might be valuable someday! But soon she took the eraser and obliterated the message so she could write many messages of her own.

School was now in session! Little Jannie had three

younger siblings and a neighborhood full of children to corral so she could play teacher. It wasn't your standard rough and tumble outdoor game, but once Little Jannie promised them a game of kickball "at recess," her pupils paid about as much attention as could be expected of wiggly young children.

Little Jannie helped them with their math sums and multiplication tables and some big, important spelling words all through the rainy winter weekends. During the summer, she held school in her backyard, where her four or five students sprawled across the backyard.

Little Jannie held her first stick of chalk before the age of 10, and, as her mother proudly tells everyone who will listen, she never let go. She grew up and taught public school children for 30 consecutive years.

Bless you Santa, for planting the seeds for her career with the simple gift of a blackboard and two small boxes of chalk!

Christmas Guard Dog

Mother wrapped piles of Christmas presents each year. She wrapped and wrapped and wrapped. At the same time, she did her best to keep us four kids out from under the tree, where we'd shake each parcel and try to guess what made that funny rattle inside.

One Christmas Eve she stationed our dog, a 12 pound curly-haired, black "Cocka-pomma-peeka-poo" with French Provincial legs (*oxymoronically named Brutus*), under the tree to "guard" the packages.

Now Brutus loved chocolate. And underneath the tree, somewhere in that mountain of gifts, there just happened to be a Whitman's Sampler, several pounds of M&Ms, and a very large milk carton of malted milk balls.

Assigned the important job of "sit and stay," Brutus dutifully burrowed beneath the branches and curled up among the colored paper-wrapped boxes. He growled a low, throaty growl at anyone who came within an arm's length of those sweet-smelling presents.

Unfortunately, when Dad arrived home, still in his white lab-type coat from work (*later Mom would blame what happened on the fact that the Veterinarian who gave shots wore a similar jacket*), no one told him that Brutus was protecting the tree.

Dad, unable to hear the warning sounds from the dog over the blaring stereo playing a rousing rendition of "Deck the Halls," made the mistake of reaching down to put a package *right next to the malt balls.* Brutus did the only thing he could think of to do. He bit him.

Dad yelled something unrepeatable and quickly pulled his hand back. We kids stood holding our breath, worried what Dad might do as he carefully examined his hand. Fortunately, no skin was broken. He turned and glowered at Mom.

"Unh-unh-unh…" Mom wagged a finger at him. "That's what happens when you try to come between the dog and his chocolate."

"The dog—," Dad spat out, but then he realized it was Christmas Eve, and his children were all within earshot. He took a deep breath, and began again in a much calmer tone, "*The dog* deserves ashes in his stocking."

"He was only doing his job, you know," said Mom.

"Don't push it," replied Dad. "Don't you dare say another word."

And for once, Mom kept quiet.

Not a Creature was Stirring

"Cathy! Wake up!" Rex paced anxiously in front of the Christmas tree. "How can you possibly sleep at a time like this?"

"It's *Catherine*," said Catherine, yawning a big satisfying yawn. "Or you can call me Cat, but please, *do not* call me Cathy." Then she stood and stretched, arching her back and bowing her neck, but being careful not to lose her balance high up on the warm fireplace mantle.

"Catherine, Cat, whatever you want," said Rex, sitting back on his haunches and tilting his head to one side as he looked up at her. "Just help me keep the watch tonight, that's all I ask."

"What's the big deal?" asked Cat, for she was, after all, naturally curious.

"Didn't you hear Mr. and Mrs. Hansen when they tucked their kids into bed tonight? This is the night that Santa's coming!"

Cat caught her balance before she laughed herself completely off the ledge. "I forgot this is your first Christmas, Rex. I hate to break this to you, Buddy, but that whole Santa thing? It's just a gimmick to get the kids to behave.

"On Christmas Eve, they're told to go to bed early so Santa can come. What actually happens is that their parents stuff the stockings and assemble bicycles and put a huge pile of gifts under the tree sometime before dawn so they can get a little rest themselves before the big day. There is no Santa, Rex. Now go ahead and get some sleep."

"No Santa?" Rex's tail abruptly stopped wagging. "I don't believe you! What about that story they read called 'T'was the Night Before Christmas'?"

"It's just a story, Rex. Trust me, I've been around long enough to know."

Rex's big brown eyes fell upon the stocking with his name embroidered on it. "No Santa?" he whispered.

"Don't worry," said Catherine, "the Hansens will most certainly put some doggie treats and a rawhide chew toy in that stocking they hung for you. And I'll be getting some fresh catnip and maybe a squeaky toy or two. It's still Christmas, Rex. We won't be left out."

Rex walked slowly to the window and laid his head on the windowsill. "I was sure if I stared at the stars long enough tonight I'd be able to pick out a sleigh sailing through the sky."

"Sorry, big guy, but it's all a myth." Cat was almost sorry she'd told him.

Rex abruptly turned and glared at Catherine. "Are you trying to trick me?" he asked. "The Hansen's have already all gone to bed and the stockings aren't filled and there aren't any bicycles under the tree either."

Cat slowly licked a paw before replying. "The family's going over to see the grandparents first thing in the morning. They had their kids tell Santa when they wrote him this year that they'd be at Granny and Gramps' for Christmas so he could leave their presents over there and make one less stop at their house here."

Cat yawned. "What a bunch of hooey!"

Rex laid down on the rag rug near the front door and put his head on his front paws. He sighed a deep sigh and closed his eyes.

Catherine was dreaming about a big gray catnip mouse when a light tinkling of bells awoke her a few hours later. She yawned and groggily glanced at the mantle clock. Three a.m. Certainly not time yet to check out her food dish. Repositioning herself on the ledge, she wasn't sure if she sensed, or actually saw, a subtle movement beneath her.

In the dim light of the twinkling tree, Cat's fur suddenly stood on end. A white-gloved hand was putting dog biscuits into Rex's stocking. Cat's eyes got big as she shook off her sleepiness and recognized, from the pictures she'd seen on a multitude of Christmas cards, the bearded man dressed all in red.

She looked quickly toward the front door. Rex, the ever-vigilant guard dog, was sound asleep.

Catherine didn't hesitate. Gathering every ounce of feline agility within her, she leaped from the mantle clear to the entryway, landing squarely on top of the snoozing Rex.

He awoke with a snort and a start, but thankfully, did not bark.

The man in red turned and took two large steps across the room. He patted Rex softly on the head before shaking his finger at Cat, but his deep blue eyes had a forgiving twinkle in them. Then he turned again, and was gone.

"That was— That was—" Rex could hardly speak. His tail began to thump wildly against the floor. He looked incredulously at Catherine.

"So I was wrong," said Cat, shrugging her feline shoulders. "I never said I was purrr-fect." She snuggled up against him on the carpet. "Merry Christmas, Rex, and to all a good night."

C-H-R-I-S-T-M-A-S Is...

Cinnamon candles held by the choir
Cranberries and popcorn to string by the fire.
Cards to address, cookies to adorn
Carolers singing the Christ Child is born.

Hallelujah! The holiest of days
Harvest completed, sing hymns of praise.
Holly to hang, as a wreath for the door
Hot buttered rum, and a holler for more!

Raisin bread pudding, relatives that come by train
Red and green stoplights look festive in the rain.
Ribbon-tied presents to give and receive
Reindeer named Rudolph for those who believe.

Invitations to parties, ice cream for the punch
Icicles to hang separately—not all in one bunch!
Incredible story of Immaculate birth
Infant from heaven, God's present to Earth.

Stuffing the stockings with Santa's surprises
Sailing the sleigh home before the sun rises.
Silver and china are set on the table
Son of God smiles at rest in the stable.

Twinkling lights hung while trimming the tree
Traveling kings, we recall there were three.

Turkey and dressing and playing with toys
Time to give thanks for our blessings and joys.

Mistletoe hanging where friend can greet friend
Mail to be opened, and more mail to send.
Mincemeat pies and Mother's home cooking
Mints to be eaten when no one is looking.

Angels adorning the tops of the trees
Aromas assaulting the nose with a tease.
Apricot preserves on apple-bran toast
Aunt Alice abustle with being our host.

Sugar and spice and peppermint sweets
Sledding at night on the snowpacked streets.
Sentimental thoughts turn to sweethearts afar
Shepherds with sheep staring up at the Star.

A Christmas Trilogy

Three Holiday One-Acts

Giving In

The Ultimatum

Walnut Garland and Airplane Parts

Giving In
The First in a Trilogy of Holiday One-Acts

Characters (*in order of appearance*):

Suzanne: Thirty-something. Wears slacks, holiday sweater, and tennis shoes.

Billy: Eight to 10 years old. Precocious little bugger. Smart, quick, and very astute. Has a jacket and stocking cap on when he first enters the house.

Pauline: Thirty-something.. Wears slacks, holiday sweater and tennis shoes. Has coat and purse when she first enters the scene.

Santa: Adult male, 50ish, wearing regular clothes with Santa hat and red scarf.

Stage Setting:

A simple "box" stage design, with the side walls angling slightly in toward the back. It is early evening on Christmas Eve. The entrance from the street is stage right. There is a mat inside the door and coat rack next to it. An exit to the kitchen and/or bedroom is modified stage left. There is a couch, stage right, and a coffee table with a poinsettia on it. An end table with a lamp, phone and phone book is downstage next to couch. There is a non-descript picture on the wall behind the sofa. A fireplace is stage left, with two stockings hanging from the mantel. A recliner/rocker or other large comfortable chair with a footstool is on each side of the fireplace. Between the fireplace and the bedroom exit is the decorated and Christmas tree along the modified wall. It has lights illuminated and a few presents beneath it. A big braided oval rug is center stage. There is a dinette table with two chairs under a window at the back wall with a half-full coffeemaker, a cup, and several rolls of wrapping paper on it. A china-type cabinet is between the table and the exit door, stage right. More cups, along with the usual dishes, are in the cabinet.

The Premise:

Suzanne has been home baking and wrapping presents this afternoon while her young son Billy has been shopping at the mall with her best friend Pauline. When the shoppers return, Suzanne discovers that Pauline has taken Billy to see Santa, and Billy has added a kitten to his Christmas wish list. This does not please Suzanne, and she firmly puts her foot down on the idea. Billy, meanwhile, is like a mouse in the corner, peeking out around the bottom corner of the modified stage left exit, making encouraging gestures outside of his mother's line of vision while Pauline works on convincing Suzanne that giving in and getting Billy a kitten for Christmas is a wonderful thing.

Giving In
The First in a Trilogy of Holiday One-Acts

There is no one onstage when the lights come up. Suzanne enters, stage left, with many rolls of Christmas wrap, some scotch tape, scissors, a couple bows, and several boxes. She drops these things on the table and starts cutting paper to fit one box. There is the sound of laughter off-stage, and she looks quickly out the window and smiles. After a short pause, the doorbell insistently rings several times.

SUZANNE: *(Laughingly calls out)* **Pull the bobbin, child, and the latch will fly up!**

Doorbell rings several more times.

SUZANNE: *(Shaking head, but smiling, calls out)* **My hands are full— you'll have to open the door yourself!**

Doorbell rings several more times.

SUZANNE: **Oh, for heaven's sake, Pauline—you've got a key, you've got my son, and the door's not even locked!** *(Laughs and remains seated, still wrapping the box)*

Doorbell rings two more times in quick succession.

SUZANNE: *(Very loud, almost exasperated)* **WOULD YOU PULL-EESE COME IN!**

Billy sticks his head in the street entrance door, stage right, and looks around, wide-eyed.

BILLY: *(Slight smirk)* **Auntie Pauline told me to ring it until you said, "Come in," so I rang the doorbell until you said exactly those words.**

SUZANNE: *(Smiling, but shaking her head)* **Billy-boy, some days you're just too smart for your britches.**

BILLY: *(Takes off stocking cap, raises up on tip-toes looking quizzically to peer at what's on the table in front of Suzanne)* **Auntie Pauline said you might be wrapping something I'm not supposed to see!**

SUZANNE: *(Smiles)* **Well, that was certainly thoughtful of Auntie Pauline, but all your presents are already under the tree.** *(Points)*

BILLY: **Oh boy! Presents!** *(Bounds into the room, leaving the door slightly ajar)* **Are they all for me?!**

SUZANNE: *(Calling out)* **Not so fast, young man! Get back there and wipe your feet!** *(Motions with thumb toward door)*

BILLY stops halfway across the room and goes back to exaggeratedly wipe his feet on the mat just inside it.

SUZANNE: **And while you're at it, you may as well hang up your hat and coat now, too.**

BILLY: *(Hurriedly)* **Yes, ma'am, right away ma'am.** *(He does as instructed, then turns first to look again at the presents, then to face her, grinning)* **Will there be anything else, ma'am?**

SUZANNE: *(Hands on hips, pretending to be annoyed)* **Yes, there is…** *(Smiles, stands, and opens her arms)* **just where's my hug?**

BILLY approaches her and they embrace.

SUZANNE: **Did you have a good time?**

BILLY: *(Smiling up at her)* **The best! Auntie Pauline let me go on the merry-go-round two times, and we had popcorn, and hot dogs, and orange juiciest and—**

SUZANNE: *(Interrupting)* **Orange juiciest?**

PAULINE enters, pushing the door open with her foot. Her arms are loaded with several tall, handled shopping bags, which she sets on the floor behind the closest chair at the table. She turns and closes the door, shrugging out of her coat as she speaks.

PAULINE: *(Laughing)* **I think he means Orange Julius.** *(She hangs up her coat.)*

SUZANNE: **Is he going to want any dinner at all tonight?**

PAULINE: **Probably not.** *(She digs in a shopping bag and comes out with a small electronic game of some sort.)* **Here you go, Billy— Your reward for being such a great kid today.**

BILLY: *(Grins happily, takes the toy and practically bounces to his room, exit stage left, calling back over his shoulder)* **Thank you, Auntie Pauline!**

SUZANNE: *(After he's gone)* **You're going to spoil him, you know.**

PAULINE: **He deserves to be spoiled a little now and then.** *(She retrieves a cup from the China cabinet and pours herself some coffee)* **So… did you get all your baking and wrapping done while we were at the mall?**

SUZANNE: **The baking, yes. The wrapping…** *(She returns to the box on the table and adds another piece of tape)…* **almost.**

PAULINE: *(Walks over to the fireplace)* **You have such a wonderful home, Suzanne.** *(Smiles. Short pause)* **It has that Norman Rockwell feeling to it.** *(Sighs)* **If you ask me, it's just about perfect.**

SUZANNE: **Just about?**

PAULINE: **Well, you know,** *(Pause)* **I was thinking that if Norman Rockwell painted a portrait of your family, he'd probably want to paint a pet into your household.**

SUZANNE: **A pet?**

PAULINE: **Uh-huh.** *(Nods, sips coffee)* **I can see it now...** *(Motions with one hand spread open as if framing the scene)* **You and Billy, here by the Christmas tree, you smiling lovingly down at him with such motherly pride as he carefully strokes a little black kitten with white paws...**

SUZANNE: **Huh-uh.** *(Shakes head)* **Not going to happen. Billy's too young to be responsible for a pet.**

PAULINE: *(Purposely avoids looking at Suzanne)* **Billy sure doesn't seem to think so...**

SUZANNE: **Pauline... is there something you're trying to tell me?**

PAULINE: **Well...** *(Pause)* **Today while we were at the mall, I took Billy to visit Santa.**

SUZANNE: **That's funny... Just a couple days ago Billy told me he doesn't believe in Santa anymore.**

(Beat) **Frankly, I was kind of relieved.**

PAULINE: **Well, I think he's hedging his bets...** *(Sips coffee)* **He wants to make sure all his bases are covered... just in case.**

SUZANNE: **And?**

PAULINE: **And he told Santa what he really wanted for Christmas this year was a kitten.**

SUZANNE: *A WHAT?!*

PAULINE: **A kitten.**

SUZANNE: *A kitten?!*

PAULINE: **Yes, for the third time, a kitten. Billy told Santa he hadn't asked his mom for one cause she thought he was too little to take care of it.**

SUZANNE: **Well, he's right about that.**

PAULINE: **Suzanne... Do you remember how old you were when you first had a pet?**

SUZANNE: **That's irrelevant—I was raised in the country.** *(She finishes the package by sticking a bow on it and placing it under the tree.)*

PAULINE: **And at just what age do you plan to start teaching him responsibility, Suze?**

SUZANNE: *(Fussing with the tree ornaments, adjusting the garland)* **Responsibility can be taught without the addition of an animal in the house.**

PAULINE: *(Sips again)* **I think a kitten would be just the thing to help Billy learn to take care of another living thing.**

SUZANNE: **Think again.** *(She returns to the table and sits with her back to the bedroom door and starts wrapping another box.)*

PAULINE: **Why are you so dead-set against the idea?**

SUZANNE: **You know who would end up taking care of it day in and day out, don't you?** *(Pauses, looks expectantly, but there is no response from Pauline)* **And *I* don't want a cat!**

PAULINE: **But Billy does.** *(She sits at the dining chair facing Suzanne and the stage left exit)*

SUZANNE: **He can wait till he's older.**

PAULINE: **Like... maybe 30?**

BILLY is seen sticking his head around the corner, down close to the floor, on his hands and knees, listening in. PAULINE can see him, but he is behind SUZANNE's back.

SUZANNE: *(Sighs)* **Maybe he'd settle for a stuffed cat.**

You know, like one of those adorable little multi-colored Beanie Babies.

BILLY is looking at PAULINE and adamantly shaking his head "no."

PAULINE: **I'm sure that's not what he had in mind, Suze.**

SUZANNE: *(Stops wrapping, tilts her head and eyes Pauline)* **How do you know? They're just as soft and cuddly, and they don't need food and water.**

PAULINE: *(Thoughtfully)* **You're right. A stuffed animal doesn't need much maintenance,** *(Shrugs)* **but it sure isn't much of a pet.**

SUZANNE: *(Continues wrapping. Furrows brow thoughtfully)* **You know, in this technological age, I bet there are stuffed animals that come with realistic sound effects...**

PAULINE: **Like purring and mewing?**

SUZANNE: *(Nods)* **Exactly.**

PAULINE: *(Snorts)* **Honestly, Suzanne... why don't you just give him a Betsy-Wetsy doll?**

Billy looks aghast, hands to cheeks, big eyes, shakes head and mouths NO!

SUZANNE: **Santa should have told him it was against the rules to carry live animals in his sleigh.**

PAULINE: **And why would Santa do that?**

SUZANNE: **Because it's unsanitary to transport animals without providing for their waste— if you know what I mean.** *(Billy's head pops out of sight as she gets up to place another finished package under the tree.)*

PAULINE: **Yes, I do know what you mean, and you have to give Billy some credit for knowing what you mean as well.**

SUZANNE: *(Frowns as she returns to the table to begin wrapping the next box)* **Just what are you saying?**

PAULINE smiles and looks innocently at the ceiling. She starts to softly hum the Christmas carol "What Child is This?"

SUZANNE: *(Glares at her)* **Come on, Pauline, spit it out.**

PAULINE: **All I'm saying is… Billy's a bright boy.**

Billy's head is again visible, and he nods and beams happily.

SUZANNE: **Yes, of course he is. No argument here.** *(Raises eyebrow)* **So what's your point?**

PAULINE: *(Draws out the first word)* **So... I happen to know he was smart enough to ask Santa to bring along some cat litter...**

SUZANNE: *(Softly echoing, eyebrows up)* **Cat litter...**

PAULINE: **And Santa said that was an excellent idea and he'd be sure to put some in his sleigh tonight.**

SUZANNE: *(Jumping up and throwing her hands in the air, Billy's head quickly disappears)* **I'll have that Santa's job! How dare him try to undermine my life like that!**

PAULINE: *(Sighs, points to chair)* **Sit down, Suzanne.** *(Waits until she does so)* **I hardly think an adorable little kitten could undermine your entire life.** *(Beat)* **Just think of it as a sweet little defenseless animal who needs a loving home.**

BILLY *is seen once again, nodding happily and giving* PAULINE *the "thumbs up" sign.*

SUZANNE: *(Sighs and shakes her head)* **You just don't understand, Pauline. You get a cat, you have to have a litter box. You have a litter box and every day *SOMEBODY* has to empty the darn thing.**

BILLY *is holding his nose and making a grimacing face.* PAULINE *starts to laugh and covers it by clearing her throat and/or coughing.*

PAULINE: **A five-minute job, tops. So what's five minutes compared to all the benefits Billy would reap by having a pet?**

SUZANNE: *(Ignores her)* **Cats can do disastrous things to upholstered furniture, you know.** *(Looks at the couch)* **You think I can afford new furniture?**

PAULINE: **That's where a scratching post comes in handy.**

BILLY rolls over on his back and uses both hands to make scratching motions in the air.

SUZANNE: *(Big sigh)* **What kind of a friend would tell my son he could have a kitten for Christmas?**

PAULINE: *(A bit defensive)* **The same kind of friend who helped you use two by fours to make sleigh runner marks out in the snow two years ago.** *(Hand on hip, pause while she squints and glares at Suzanne)* **The same kind of friend who got that deer hoof from her neighbor who hunts so we could make reindeer tracks for Billy to find on Christmas morning.**

Billy's eyebrows go up and he looks genuinely surprised.

SUZANNE: **Yeah, and who was it who miscounted those tracks?** *(She starts to laugh)* **Remember? We had 35 hoof prints out there and Billy counted**

**them and wanted to know why there weren't 32
or 36 cause reindeer have four legs.**

PAULINE: *(Laughing now too)* **And who thought fast
and explained to him that Rudolph must have
been limping from working so hard all night!**
(More laughter erupts from both of them)

SUZANNE: *(Catching her breath)* **That was quick
thinking, all right.**

PAULINE: **Who knew he'd learned his multiplication
tables already?**

SUZANNE: *(Grins)* **He's a smart kid, alright, but we
proved we're still just a little bit smarter!**

PAULINE: **Face it, girlfriend, Lucy and Ethel's got
nothing on us!**

*SUZANNE leans forward and gives PAULINE a "high
five." Then she stands and BILLY quickly disappears from
the floor of the doorway.*

SUZANNE: **You want some fruitcake?** *(She exits, stage
left, where Billy has been seen throughout, without
waiting for an answer.)*

PAULINE: *(Calling out)* **Is it the same one you served
me last year?** *(She turns in her chair and shuffles
through the bags behind her but takes nothing out)*

SUZANNE returns with two plates. A piece of fruitcake and a fork are on each one. She places one in front of PAULINE and sits. They each take a forkful in silence, chew, swallow, look at each other with raised eyebrows.

SUZANNE: *(Takes a sip of coffee. Licks her lips.)* **It's not so bad, really.**

PAULINE: *(Shaking her head)* **No, it's definitely better than last year's.**

SUZANNE: **Would be better, I think, if it had just a little more time to ferment.**

PAULINE: **Or if we had some brandy to soak it in.**

SUZANNE: **For about a week.**

PAULINE: **No...** *(Shakes her head)* **at least a month. Bare minimum.** *(They both laugh. Pause. She clears her throat)* **So, about Billy's kitten...**

BILLY appears again on the floor grinning like a Cheshire cat from ear to ear, nodding.

SUZANNE: **Haven't you been listening? Billy is *NOT* getting a kitten.**

PAULINE: **I thought you liked cats.**

SUZANNE: *(Sarcastically)* **The only way I like cats is barbecued.**

BILLY looks horrified, wide-eyed, he presses open hands to cheeks again just as the kid did in "Home Alone."

PAULINE: *SUZANNE!!*

SUZANNE: *(Agitated, she stands and grasps the edge of the table. Billy pops his head back out of sight.)* **Now I suppose you'll turn me in to the NAACP.** (Pronounced "N-double A-C-P)

PAULINE: *(Softly)* **I think you mean the A-S-P-C-A.**

SUZANNE: *(Exaggeratedly)* **What—ever.** *(Shakes her head, exhales sharply)* **Excuse me for a moment, will you? I need to go tuck Billy into bed.** *(Exits)*

As soon as Suzanne is out of the room, Pauline digs back into the shopping bags behind her chair and retrieves a scratching post, a small bag of litter, some kitten nibbles, a few free-standing cat batting toys, rolling yarn balls and/or a catnip mouse. Some items have bows on them. It takes several trips to place all these gifts under the tree, and then she steps back to admire her handiwork. She places a hand on her hip and is smiling a big, self-satisfied smile when Suzanne returns and catches her in the act.

SUZANNE: **Pauline! What, exactly, do you think you're doing?**

PAULINE: *(Sheepishly)* **Just in case Santa *DOES* come through, I thought it might be nice if you had**

some of these things on hand.

SUZANNE: **Why do you want to get Billy's hopes up?**
(She starts to gather up the cat toys)

PAULINE: *(Goes to fireplace and adjusts the stockings or fidgets with the items on the mantel)* **Billy wants a pet to care for, Suze. He has his heart set on having a warm and fuzzy little animal who depends on him.**

SUZANNE: **You mean another little life that depends on *ME*, don't you?**

PAULINE: **Let him show you how responsible and grown up he can be.**

SUZANNE: *(Sits on the floor under the tree with her arms full of cat toys.)* **You know, sometimes I wish he'd never grow up.**

PAULINE: *(Sits in rocker or chair nearest Suzanne and leans forward earnestly, speaks softly)* **I do know... Believe me... But you can't treat him like a baby forever...**

SUZANNE: **Things are perfect between us just the way they are. I wouldn't want my expectations over his pet ownership to destroy the special bond we have.**

PAULINE: **Just take it slow. Teach him step-by-step.**

SUZANNE: *(Considering, echoes)* **Step-by-step.**

PAULINE: **He's a fast learner—we both know that. Before long you won't even have to remind him when it's time to change the water dish.**

SUZANNE: *(Ruefully)* ***AND*** **the cat box…**

PAULINE: *(Ignores her)* **Consider it a compliment… Billy wants to share what he's learned from you about nurturing with a helpless little animal.**

SUZANNE: *(Pause)* **So… you really think taking care of a kitten would be good for him?**

PAULINE: **Yes I do, Suzanne. He's a great kid, but he's an only child.**

SUZANNE: *(Defensively)* **Hey, it's not my fault his father didn't want to stick around and be a Dad.**

PAULINE: **That's not what I was getting at, and you know it.** *(Pause, then softly)* **I bet Billy will surprise you.**

SUZANNE: *(Sighs again, considering. Shakes her head. Starts putting the items back under the tree. Looks at her watch.)* **What would surprise me is if there's a pet shop anywhere in this county that's still open on Christmas Eve.**

PAULINE: *(Surprised)* **You're really giving in?**

SUZANNE: **As much as I hate to admit it, Pauline, your arguments make sense. So yes, I'm giving in.**

PAULINE: **You won't regret it, Suze.**

SUZANNE: **I already regret us not having this conversation a couple days ago.** *(Pause)* **What am I supposed to tell Billy tomorrow? That Santa left him an I.O.U. for a kitten?**

PAULINE: *(Smiles)* **Suzanne, do you believe in miracles?**

SUZANNE: **Miracles, yes. Finding a kitten at this hour? I doubt it.** *(She crosses downstage to the phone, picks up the phone book and starts flipping through the yellow pages.)*

PAULINE: **Then let me put it another way.** *(She stands and takes a deep breath)* **Do you believe in Santa Claus?**

SUZANNE: **Get serious.**

PAULINE: **I am serious**. *(She goes to the window)* **Come here a minute.**

Suzanne looks puzzled, but sets down the phone book and joins Pauline at the window.

PAULINE: **Remember back when you were a kid?**

SUZANNE: *(Sarcastically)* **It wasn't *THAT* long ago...**

PAULINE: *(She puts an arm around Suzanne's shoulders)* **Remember standing at the window and watching for Santa Claus?**

SUZANNE: *(Softly smiles)* **I remember staring at the stars so hard I thought I could actually see them move.** *(Beat)* **I was sure if I believed with all my heart and stood there long enough, I'd just have to see Santa fly by on his sleigh.** *(Wistfully after short pause)* **I'd just have to.**

PAULINE: **So I repeat: Do you believe in Santa Claus?**

SUZANNE: *(Sighs)* **Get to the point, Pauly.**

PAULINE: **Close your eyes.**

SUZANNE: *(Warily)* **Why?**

PAULINE: **Just humor me, will you?**

SUZANNE: *(Still warily)* **For how long?**

PAULINE: **Until I say you can open them.**

SUZANNE: *(Sighs again)* **Very well. But first I'm going to get comfortable.** *(She crosses to recliner and sits, putting her feet up)* **Okay, my eyes are**

closed. *(Beat)* **Wake me in the morning.**

PAULINE goes to the outside door, opens it and motions dramatically for someone to hurry and "come here." SANTA, a middle-aged man wearing a Santa hat and red scarf, enters carrying a cat carrier. He slowly and exaggeratedly tiptoes over to the tree, gently sets the pet carrier down and tiptoes back out. PAULINE closes the door softly behind him.

From the floor by the bedroom exit, BILLY grins happily and extends both his "thumbs up"— way up.

As the lights dim, we hear a distinctive "meowing."

CURTAIN CALL

The Ultimatum
The Second in a Trilogy of Holiday One-Acts

<u>**Characters**</u> (*in order of appearance*):

Grandma Maybelle (Henry's mother): Typical granny. Gray hair in bun. Glasses on end of nose. Fuzzy slippers. Spends the entire play sitting in the recliner/rocker between the fireplace and the Christmas tree, knitting. She misses nothing, and has plenty to say about what she observes.

Abigail (Mom): Think Harriet Nelson. Early 40s. Strives to preserve the peace and keep things running smoothly. Family and traditions are very dear to her.

Jessie: Younger female sibling, 12. The hand-me-down daughter. Observes her older sister and tries to emulate her.

William: Younger male sibling, 7 1/2. Still desperately wants to believe in Santa. He is the coddled "baby" of the family. "Cute" is his best attribute.

Henry (Dad): Think Ozzie Nelson. Non-descript early middle-aged male. Glasses. Wears classy Christmas suspenders and/or holiday tie.

Samantha: Teen-aged daughter, 16. Long hair, definite attitude. Like most teens, she has an answer for everything.

Santa: Adult male, will be heard but not seen onstage.

Stage Setting:

Same layout as in "Giving In." Now there are five stockings hanging on the mantel. A quantity of red and green paper "Christmas chains" strung on the tree, along the mantel, looped on the top of picture frames and across the China hutch. More packages have been added beneath the tree. The wrapping paper on the dining table is gone; the poinsettia has replaced it. A crèche is on the coffee table next to a stack of board game boxes. Grandma's yarn bag is on the floor beside the recliner between the fireplace and the tree. It is early evening on Christmas Eve. Exits and furniture remain the same.

The Premise:

Teen-aged Samantha has made it perfectly clear: She wants nothing but a car for Christmas. If she can't have a car, then she doesn't want anything at all. Henry, her father, is just as firm in his resolve *not* to get her a car. A story of generational love, laughter, and growing pains.

The Ultimatum
The Second in a Trilogy of Holiday One-Acts

As lights come up, Grandma is in the recliner, knitting. She is humming "Silent Night." After a few lines of the song, there is the sound of stomping feet on the porch. Abigail, Jessica and William enter wearing winter coats.

ABIGAIL: *(She takes off her coat and hangs it on the coat rack by the door.)* **Come on kids, let's get your coats hung up.**

JESSICA does so, but WILLIAM is having difficulty with this coat zipper. ABIGAIL moves to assist him, but he pulls abruptly away.

WILLIAM: **I can do it all by myself!**

ABIGAIL: *(Puts her hands up in surrender and backs away)* **I know you can, sweetheart.**

JESSICA sits on sofa and begins setting up a board game on the coffee table. WILLIAM succeeds in shucking out of his coat, which he throws on a chair, and sits across from JESSICA on the floor. ABIGAIL hangs his coat.

ABIGAIL: **You should have come with us, Maybelle. You would have enjoyed all the festive music.**

GRANDMA: *(Nodding as she continues to knit)* **I'm sure it was just lovely Abigail, but I need every spare minute to finish all the scarves I promised for the annual ladies' church bazaar fundraiser in January. You know how they all count on me.**

ABIGAIL: **Yes, and they'll be delighted with however many you end up giving them, Maybelle.**

GRANDMA: **Yes, but a promise is a promise.**

ABIGAIL joins JESSICA and WILLIAM at the coffee table, where they are rolling dice and moving board pieces. They will continue to do this throughout much of the remainder of the evening. HENRY comes into the room from stage left.

HENRY: **I thought I heard my caroling angels return!** *(He crosses to Abigail, who is sitting on the couch, and gives her a kiss on the cheek. He ruffles William's hair.)* **How was the party, Abigail?**

ABIGAIL: *(Smiles)* **We could have used a few more male voices.**

WILLIAM: **I'm a male voice...** *(Frowns, looks at Abigail)* **aren't I?**

JESSICA: *(Snorts)* **Not yet, you're not.**

GRANDMA: **Now you just hush yourself, Jessie. William has a fine young male voice.**

HENRY: *(Pulls a dining chair up to the end of the coffee table to join them. He looks around)* **Where's Samantha? Didn't she go with you?**

ABIGAIL: **She went with us, but she wanted to hang out with her school chums at the mall afterward. She said she'd be able to catch a ride home later with one of her friends.**

JESSICA: **You mean her *boyfriend*...**

WILLIAM: *(Singsong)* **Sammy has a boyfriend! Sammy has a boyfriend!**

HENRY: *(Aghast)* **Samantha has a boyfriend?** *(He looks at Abigail)* **Did you know about this?**

ABIGAIL: *(Nods)* **His name is Brian.**

HENRY: **Brian? I don't know any of her friends named Brian. When did this happen?** *(He runs a hand through his hair and looks from Abigail to Maybelle and back)*

ABIGAIL: **She's 16, Henry—**

JESSICA: *(Interrupting excitedly)* **And I'm almost 13,**

Dad. I'll be a teenager in just two more months!

HENRY: *(Shaking his head)* **Don't remind me…**

WILLIAM: **And me!** *(Bouncing up an down)* **I'm seven and a half!**

ABIGAIL: *(Sweetly, almost baby-talk)* **Who could forget Mommy's little man?**

JESSICA: *(Under her breath)* **I probably could…**

Before either parent can chastise JESSICA, SAMANTHA bounds into the house. She is bubbling with happiness, which seems to surprise most everyone. She hangs up her coat gives everyone a big cheesy grin.

SAMANTHA: *(Genuinely happy)* **We're all here…** *(She sighs, and continues brightly)* **Just like a Norman Rockwell Christmas Eve family portrait.**

ABIGAIL: **My, aren't you in a good mood tonight!**

HENRY: *(Smiling)* **Nice to see my eldest daughter's got a better attitude now than earlier today.**

JESSICA: *(Smugly)* **She's also got a whisker burn rash on her chin from kissing her boyfriend—**

SAMANTHA: *(Hand flying to her chin to check it out)* **You little rat! You've been spying on me!** *(Angrily imploring)* **Mom! Dad! Can't a person get any**

privacy around here?!

SAMANTHA makes a hasty retreat to her bedroom, exit stage left. We hear a door slam.

GRANDMA: **Now *that's* the Sammy we all know and love.**

ABIGAIL: **Jessica, go apologize to your sister.**

JESSICA: **Do I *have to*?**

HENRY: **Yes, young lady, you do… It *IS* Christmas Eve, after all. You don't want to get on the "naughty" list at this late hour, do you?** *(He points to the Exit)* **Now march!**

JESSICA slowly drags herself out of the room, making a face back over her shoulder.

WILLIAM: *(Singsong voice)* **Sammy and Brian, sittin' in a tree, K-I-S-S-I-N-G.**

GRANDMA: **William Michael! It's not too late to email Santa and tell him you've blown it.**

WILLIAM: *(Hangs his head)* **Yes, Grammy.**

HENRY: *(Looking toward the bedroom)* **It's pretty quiet in there.**

ABIGAIL: *(Calling)* **Samantha? Jessica? Come back**

out and join the family.

The girls return. JESSICA takes her place back on the sofa. SAMANTHA has a pair of pantyhose in her hand. She goes to the mantel and hangs them next to the other stockings.

ABIGAIL: *(Admonishing)* **Samantha!**

JESSICA: *(Sighs)* **I wish I was old enough to wear pantyhose.**

ABIGAIL: *(Correcting her grammar)* **That's I wish I WERE, Jessie.**

JESSICA: *(Shrugs)* **Was, were, what's the difference? I'm still treated like a baby around here.**

GRANDMA: *(Looking at the row of stockings and nodding)* **That may be a bit optimistic, honey, but what the heck.**

HENRY: *(Raises eyebrows)* **Samantha, I don't know why you're even bothering to hang up a stocking.**

ABIGAIL: *(To Henry, in a hushed voice)* **Henry**—(*Pats his hand*) **It's Christmas Eve.**

HENRY: *(Authoritatively)* **I'm well aware of that, Abigail.** *(Raises eyebrows and sighs)* **And I'm also aware that our eldest daughter here gave me an ultimatum a few weeks ago. An ultimatum in** which she declared that if she couldn't have what she really wanted for Christmas, then she wanted nothing at all.

JESSICA: *(Quizzically looking at the adults)* **What's an ultimatum?**

GRANDMA: **Your sister asked Santa for a car, Jessica.**

JESSICA and WILLIAM: *(Astounded)* **A CAR!!??**

SAMANTHA: *(To Henry)* **It's not like everyone in the family wouldn't benefit from me having a car.**

JESSICA: *(Warming to the idea, eyebrows arcing up)* **And then she could leave it to me when she goes to college.**

SAMANTHA: *(Scowls at Jessica, then sits in the vacant chair next to Maybelle, but speaks to Henry)* **I'd be able to run lots of errands for Mom and Grandma, take Jessica to soccer practice, and drive little Will to T-Ball.**

GRANDMA: *(Nodding)* **Those sound like real timesavers for your folks, all right, Sammy.**

SAMANTHA: *(Finding an ally, turns to Grandma)* **I'd also be able to get myself to and from my babysitting jobs.**

HENRY: **And who would pay the insurance?**

SAMANTHA: **I've got better than a "B" average, so I'd get a discount.**

HENRY: *(Clears throat)* **That doesn't answer my question, Samantha.**

SAMANTHA: *(Pouting, folds arms across chest)* **My car insurance wouldn't cost as much as those braces Jessica's getting next month.**

JESSICA: *(Hand flies to cover mouth, shrieks)* **MOM!**

ABIGAL: *(Calmly)* **Those braces are a necessity, Samantha. We're not picking favorites here.**

WILLIAM: *(Squinting at Abigail, says softly)* **Hey... I thought *I* was your favorite.**

ABIGAIL: *(Pats him on the hand)* **Hush, dear... please.**

HENRY: **And how would you keep those grades up if you were out running around in your car every afternoon?**

SAMANTHA: *(Smugly)* **I only need a "B" average, Dad—that's a 3.0—and right now I have a 3.3, so—no worries!**

HENRY: *(Scowls)* **I'm not talking about skating by on bare minimums, young lady. You have college admissions to think about.**

SAMANTHA: *(Annoyed, under her breath)* **That's not till next year.**

HENRY: *(Also annoyed)* **You haven't answered either of my last two questions, Samantha.**

SAMANTHA: *(Dramatically sighs)* **Ok, Ok… It's like this, see—***(leans forward in chair, intense)* **I'll actually have lots *more* time for homework, cause I won't be stuck riding home on the activities bus every day.**

GRANDMA: *(Pipes up)* **How's that, Sammy?**

SAMANTHA: *(Glad to elaborate)* **It takes almost two hours to get home when I ride that stupid bus cause it has to go all over the county dropping kids off.**

GRANDMA: *(Nodding thoughtfully)* **I guess I'm a little slow on the uptake today, Samantha. Just spell it out.**

SAMANTHA: **Well, Grammy, if I drive straight home I can make it in just 15 minutes.**

ABIGAIL and HENRY: *(Shocked)* ***FIFTEEN* minutes?!**

SAMANTHA: *(Sighs)* **Ok… make it twenty.**

JESSICA: *(Eagerly)* **If I can't have Sammy's car when**

she leaves for college, can I one of my very own when I'm 16?

WILLIAM: **Me too! Me too!** *(Bouncing up and down)* **I want a green one! Vrrrooom! Vrrrooom!**

HENRY: *(Sighs, rolls eyes)* **Let me make myself perfectly clear: Samantha is *NOT* getting a car.**

GRANDMA: **I dunno, Henry, I think she's making a pretty strong argument for it.**

HENRY: **Mother, you stay out of this.**

ABIGAIL: *(Cheerily changing the subject)* **Why don't we all just calm down and sing some of our favorite Christmas songs?**

SAMANTHA: *(Quickly belting it out solo and pointedly)* **I'm dreaming of a CAR for Christmas…**

ABIGAIL: **That's enough, Samantha.** *(Short pause)* **How about "Deck the Halls"?**

JESSICA: **My friend Karen Hall hates that one. She says it's politically incorrect to sing it around her, or her family, or anyone else named Hall.**

HENRY: *(Looks at Jessica, opens mouth to say something, but turns to Samantha)* **Ok, Samantha, just supposing you *WERE* going to get a car—**

SAMANTHA: *(Pumps fist)* **YES!**

HENRY: **Just supposing…** *(Beat)* **Have you done any research on the make or model, the estimated mileage and so forth?**

SAMANTHA: *(Nodding quickly and excitedly)* **As a matter of fact, I have!** *(She beams, and it all comes out in a rush)* **Down on the corner of 196ᵗʰ and 44ᵗʰ—there's this used car lot—and they've got this really pretty little blue and white Mustang—**

HENRY: *(Loudly interrupts)* **A MUSTANG?!**

SAMANTHA: *(Ducks her head)* **Oops…**

GRANDMA: *(Laughing calls out)* **Strategic error, Sammy, sweetie—Retreat and regroup!**

HENRY opens his mouth to say something to SAMANTHA, but ABIGAIL quickly interjects before he can speak.

ABIGAIL: *(Quickly)* **Ok, everybody, all together now—** *(She sings)* **Up on the housetop, reindeers pause…** *(She motions for the others to join in, and they reluctantly do so, gathering momentum as they sing)*

ALL: **…Out jumps good old Santa Claus, Down through the chimney with lots of toys, all for the little ones' Christmas joys.** *(Abigail tousles William's hair fondly)* **Ho, ho, ho, who wouldn't**

go, (*Henry gets up and moves toward the fireplace, still singing along*) **Ho, ho, ho, who wouldn't go, Up on the housetop** *They all snap their fingers three times with the words*) **Click, Click, Click, Down through the chimney with Old St. Nick.**

Henry reaches into his pocket and pulls out a set of keys on a key ring. He drops them with a flourish into the pantyhose.

SAMANTHA: (*Shrieks with joy as she dashes for her stocking*) **Oh Dad! Oh Dad! I knew you wouldn't let me down!** (*She rips the pantyhose from the mantel and takes the keys out. She looks at them, confused*) **Dad?**

HENRY: (*Smiles brightly*) **They're keys to the family station wagon, Sammy.**

SAMANTHA: (*Stares at the keys in disbelief*) **Keys to the station wagon?**

HENRY: (*Nods, puts a hand on her shoulder*) **You knew we couldn't afford another car in the family—**

SAMANTHA: (*Still looking at the keys in her hand, says softly*) **The *station wagon*?**

HENRY: (*Continues as if he hasn't been interrupted*)— **so I got you a key ring with your name on it and your own set of car keys.**

SAMANTHA: *(Anger and disgust, speaks loudly)* **The station wagon?!! Seriously? Oh, DAD!** *(She runs to her room, pantyhose and keys still in hand, and slams door again)*

ABIGAIL: *(Frowning)* **Henry, was that really necessary?**

HENRY: **She needs to learn the value of a dollar, Abigail.**

ABIGAIL: *(Standing, speaking between clenched teeth)* **Kids, go get into your PJs now.**

JESSICA: *(Groans)* **Ah, Mom…**

GRANDMA: *(Quietly)* **Do as she says, honey.**

JESSICA: *(Imploring, drawing out the words)* **But Grammy, I'm almost 13. Can't I stay up a little later?**

GRANDMA: *(Quietly)* **Your mother wishes so speak to your father privately, Jessie… Now hop along!**

ABIGAIL: **Yes, both of you—Hop to it! Go put on your PJs and then together we'll all read "T'was the Night Before Christmas" when you're ready for bed.**

JESSICA: *(Resigned)* **Ok,** *(sighs)* **we'll go…** *(She takes William by the hand to lead him away)*

ABIGAIL: *(Relenting slightly)* **Jess—**

JESSICA: *(Turning hopefully)* **Yes?**

ABIGAIL: **You're right, honey. You're almost 13.** *(Stands and hugs them together.* **That's old enough to be the one to read the book this year.** *(Smiles)* **Now Scoot! Go get into your jammies—both of you.**

JESSICA and WILLIAM then leave the room. ABIGAIL turns to HENRY. She puts her hands on hips and is obviously seething.

GRANDMA: *(Raises eyebrows)* **You want that I should leave the room?**

ABIGAIL: *(Measuring her words)* **No, Maybelle, you sit right there.**

GRANDMA: **Good. I didn't want to miss the show.** *(Nods thoughtfully)* **It's just not the same when I only get the audio by listening through the walls.**

Henry looks at Maybelle, obviously amused, but says nothing.

ABIGAIL: *(Sits on the couch and pats the seat next to her.)* **Henry? I think it's time we had a little chat.**

HENRY obligingly joins ABIGAIL on the sofa. Grandma stops her knitting for the first time all night and eagerly leans forward, so she won't miss a word.

ABIGAIL: **Henry, do you even remember being 16?**

HENRY: *(Rolls eyes and sighs)* **Your point, Abby?**

ABIGAIL: **You remember how you wanted so much to be able to drive everywhere, anytime you wanted?**

HENRY: **Nobody ever gave *ME* a car...**

GRANDMA: *(Interrupting)* **But our neighbor, old Jim Peterson, used to let you drive his old flatbed hay truck whenever he wasn't using it on his farm.**

ABIGAIL: *(Pointedly)* **I think I can handle this, Maybelle.**

GRANDMA: **Right. No problem.** *(Nods)* **Just wanted to put my two cents in.** *(Still nodding)* **I was *there*, you know.**

HENRY: **So noted, Mother.** *(Turns to Abigail)* **If Samantha wants to drive Mr. Peterson's old flatbed, I'll see if I can arrange it.**

ABIGAIL: *(Peers at him, pause)* **Henry Richard Newton, don't you want life to be a bit better for your daughter than the way you had it as a kid?**

HENRY: *(Sighs)* **I take it that's rhetorical.**

GRANDMA: *(Back to knitting)* **Ah, he didn't have it so bad, Abby. He made it all up when he told Samantha he had to walk five miles to school and back each day in two feet of snow.**

ABIGAIL: *(Smiling, to Maybelle)* **Sammy's a smart girl, Maybelle. I think she figured out he was telling a tale when he said it was uphill both ways.**

HENRY: (Scowling) **Hold on a second. Why am I getting ganged up on? I'm not the bad guy here. It's a matter of financial responsibility;** *(Emphatically)* **we can't afford another car.**

ABIGAIL: *(Purses lips)* **I think we can, Henry.**

HENRY: *(Raises eyebrows)* **You do?**

ABIGAIL: **Yes I do. I've been juggling the budget a little, and I think I can squeeze a few more dollars out of our regular monthly expenses.**

GRANDMA: *(Happily nodding)* **Atta girl, Abigail, you can do it! Just squee-eeze Sammy's car bucks right outta those turnips!**

ABIGAIL and HENRY both look at her confused, but shrug it off.

HENRY: **And you think you can do this without having to cut cardboard soles to put into the**

worn-out shoes of our children?

GRANDMA: **Hey! I only did that once, I swear!**

ABIGAIL: *(Ignoring Grandma, still speaking to Henry)* **If we waited until just after the holidays I really think we could find her a safe and reliable little car we can easily afford.**

GRANDMA: **We'll make it a family project!**

HENRY: *(Sighs, resigned)* **Okay.** *(Nods)* **So then, what are we going to put in her stocking tonight, an I.O.U.?**

ABIGAIL: **As we've already mentioned, Samantha's a big girl, Henry, and she's smart. She'll understand.**

HENRY and GRANDMA nod, thinking it over JESSICA appears in the doorway in a flannel nightgown with WILIAM in tow.

JESSICA: **Is it safe to come out now?**

WILLIAM, in pajamas, happily dances over to HENRY, climbs up into his lap and gives him a hug.

HENRY: **Well, at least somebody around here still loves me.**

ABIGAIL: **We all love you, Henry.** *(Sighs)* **It's just that**

sometimes we have to work extra hard to get
through to you.

WILLIAM: *(Looks up at him)* **When are we going to
put the carrots out for Santa's reindeer?**

GRANDMA: **Carrots for the reindeer? Why, I never
heard of such a thing!**

JESSICA: **The reindeer need to keep their strength up
for the long trip, Grandma, and reindeer don't
eat cookies.**

WILLIAM: *(Nodding)* **Yeah, reindeer don't eat cookies.
Cookies aren't good for them.** *(Hunches his
shoulders and giggles)* **But cookies are good for
little boys!** *(Nods and rubs his tummy)* **Yum!**

*SAMANTHA appears hesitantly at the doorway. She is
still fully dressed and is holding the book "T'was the Night
Before Christmas." ABIGAIL motions for her to join them
and they all get comfortable. SAMANTHA hands the book
to JESSICA.*

SAMANTHA: **Here, Jessie. I think I heard it was your
turn to read this tonight.**

JESSICA: *(Sarcastically)* **Oh, you think you heard that,
huh?** *(She smiles and takes the book)* **I think I could
almost recite it by heart.**

ABIGAIL: *(Nods)* **The reading of this story is a**

tradition that's been handed down in thousands, if not millions, of families all over the world.

HENRY: *(Smiles and puts his arm around JESSICA)* **In other words, Jess, you're** *supposed* **to have it almost memorized.**

GRANDMA: *(Grins and nods)* **I'll start!** *(Clears throat)* **T'was the night before Christmas…**

HENRY: **And all through the house…**

ABIGAIL: **Not a creature was stirring…**

JESSICA: **Not even a mouse…**

WILLIAM stands and scrunches his body up as if he is a little mouse, hands together like little paws in front of him, and goes scurrying around the room, while his indulgent family looks on. There is the sound of a car horn beeping twice… BEEP-BEEP. WILLIAM does his little mouse-scurry over to the window, pulls the shade back, stands on tip-toes and looks out.

WILLIAM: *(Excitedly)* **It's Santa!** *(Extremely wiggly-excited)* **It's Santa! It's SANTA! Come look!** *(Holds curtain back)* **It's Santa—and he's driving a little blue and white car!**

Everyone, except GRANDMA, who smiles while she continues to knit, is up and running to the window. SAMANTHA takes a quick look, SHRIEKS WITH JOY, grabs her coat off the rack and bolts out the door.

JESSICA: **OMG!** *(Letters spelled out O-M-G)* **It's a MUSTANG!**

HENRY, ABIGAIL and GRANDMA all quizzically look at each other with a palms-up "beats me" "I know nothing about this" kind of shrug and shake their heads.

SANTA: *(Offstage, in booming Santa voice)* **Happy Christmas to all, and to all a good night!**

Lights dim—CURTAIN CALL

Walnut Garland and Airplane Parts
The Third in a Trilogy of Holiday One-Acts

<u>**Characters**</u> (*in order of appearance*):

Julia Barnett: Mid-fifties. She is the eldest of the siblings. Single. Wears nice slacks and blouse, shoes with slight heel. Wears full over-the-head Christmas kitchen apron as play begins.

Laurie Smith: Julia's just slightly younger sister. Casually dressed, jeans and holiday sweater. Tennis shoes. Arrives in light windbreaker jacket.

Brian Smith: Laurie's husband. Dressed in jeans and flannel or other work shirt. Arrives in "work jacket," something like Carhartt's, and stocking cap. Light work boots.

Jack Barnett: Julia and Laurie's slightly younger brother. Wears slacks and dress shirt, perhaps with cufflinks, tie, polished shoes. Arrives in full outdoor winter coat and hat and scarf and gloves.

Karen Barnett: Jack's wife. Appearances are everything to her. Dress or skirt, too much jewelry, heels. Arrives dressed for frigid outdoors. Carries purse.

Rick Thomas: Adult male, Mother's lawyer, arrives in business suit, Santa hat, and red scarf. (*This man could be the Santa for all three plays*)

Stage Setting:

Same layout as in "Giving In." Now there is only one stocking hanging on the mantel and no presents under the tree. The paper chains are gone, replaced by gold or silver garland. The dinette table is now a larger round dining table and a linen tablecloth has been placed over it, a candelabra is in the center. The table, complete with wine glasses, is set for six. Several heavy dining chairs replace the lighter ones. The buffet is now a full beverage bar, with decanters and glasses. The crèche is still on the coffee table, now surrounded with cotton "snow" and a few angel figurines. The games are gone. There's a bowl of mixed nuts and one of Vernell's buttermints also on the coffee table. It is early evening on Christmas Eve.

The Premise:

It is the first Christmas after their mother's passing, and the siblings have gathered at the elder daughter's house for dinner on Christmas Eve. Tension is high until they begin going through a photo album and sharing stories of Christmases past. An unexpected guest arrives, and they realize the greatest gift of all.

Walnut Garland and Airplane Parts
The Third in a Trilogy of Holiday One-Acts

There is no one onstage as lights come up. After a beat, doorbell rings. JULIA enters, stage left, dressed in "nice" slacks and blouse, but with a full-length holiday apron tied around her waist.

JULIA: **Coming! Coming! Just a moment, please!**

She moves across the stage, untying the apron as she goes, quickly stashing it behind the couch and glancing in the mirror by the door to fuss with her hair for a moment. The doorbell rings a second time, and JULIA plants a forced smile on her face as she swings the door open wide.

JULIA: **Come in! Come in! Merry Christmas!**

JULIA steps aside, and LAURIE and BRIAN enter, dressed casually, wearing light winter coats. LAURIE carries a wrapped package, and once she spies the tree, crosses stage to place it gingerly underneath.

LAURIE: *(Turning)* **What a nice place you have!**

BRIAN: *(Nods)* **Not a lot of parking out there, though. We had to leave our car in the lot at the bottom of the hill and hike up.**

JULIA: *(Ignores both remarks)* **Here, let me take your coats.** *(They shuck off their jackets, Julia takes them and quickly hangs them on the coat rack by the door)* **Sit down! Please, sit down!** *(Motions to the couch)*

LAURIE and BRIAN sit, but they are obviously uncomfortable, still looking about. JULIA perches on the edge of a dining chair, all are at a loss for words.

BRIAN: *(At last)* **Well... Uh... Here we are...***(Brightens and rubs hand together as if an idea suddenly comes to him)* **Got anything to drink?**

JULIA: *(Jumping up)* **Oh yes! Yes, of course! Where *are* my manners?** *(She moves to the buffet by the door where there are several decanters and glasses)* **Uh... what would you like?**

LAURIE: *(Thinks a moment. Surveys bottles on buffet)* **You got any white wine?**

BRIAN: **I'll take a bourbon and water.** *(Rubs his hands briskly together again)* **That'll take the chill off.**

JULIA: *(Fixing their drinks)* **Have you heard from Jack**

and Karen? I thought they'd be here by now.

BRIAN: *(Looks at watch)* Maybe they got held up in Christmas Eve traffic.

LAURIE: *(Hopefully, brightly)* Or maybe they're not coming!

JULIA: *(Hands drinks to them)* Now, now, it's time we all learned to play nice.

LAURIE: *(Holds wine glass, doesn't sip, tilts head, eyes Julia)* Why?

JULIA: *(Scowls)* Because Mother would want it that way, that's why.

BRIAN: *(Takes a sip and smacks lips)* Oh yeah, this is what I'm talking about—you got the good stuff!

LAURIE: *(To Brian)* You best watch that "good stuff" so I don't have to drive us both home.

BRIAN: *(Scowling, mocking)* Yes, dear.

JULIA: Well… dinner's already in the oven, but I better go check on it. Please make yourselves at home. *(Exits, stage left)*

LAURIE: *(Looks around and shrugs)* So how are we supposed to do that?

BRIAN: *(Takes another deep sip)* **I don't know about you, but I'm starting to feel right at home here.** *(Leans forward and absentmindedly takes a handful of nuts from the bowl on the coffee table and pops a few into his mouth)*

LAURIE: *(Takes a swipe at his hand)* **Don't eat those! You'll ruin your dinner!**

BRIAN: *(Shakes head)* **Notta chance! I've been starving myself all day. Your sister is the best darn cook in the whole darn family.**

LAURIE: *(Glowers at him)* **And what's *THAT* suppose to mean?**

Before BRIAN can answer, the doorbell rings again. They raise eyebrows and both turn to look at the door, but neither makes a move.

JULIA: *(Calls from offstage)* **Could one of you get that, please?**

LAURIE and BRIAN point to each other, but finally LAURIE rolls her eyes and gets up to go to the door. She opens it, and KAREN and JACK enter. They are dressed for very cold weather—coats, scarves, hats, gloves. JACK carries a very elegant foil-wrapped package; KAREN carries a nice purse.

LAURIE: *(Peers at her bundled-up brother Jack)* **Is there anyone I know in there?**

JACK: *(Laughing)* **And a Merry Christmas, to you, too, Sis.**

LAURIE: *(Tilts head, squints at him quizzically)* **You haven't called me Sis since we were kids.** *(Beat, then continues suspiciously)* **You must want something.**

JACK moves to hug her, but she is stiff and leaves her hands at her sides, stepping back to avoid his embrace. He doesn't press the issue.

KAREN: **Ok, ok, enough already with all this sibling sentimentality...** *(To Jack)* **Is anyone going to help me get my coat off?**

JACK: *(Looks around, grins sheepishly and shrugs)* **I guess she means me...**

JACK sets package on table, dutifully helps KAREN remove her winter attire, and takes his own off as well. Compared to BRIAN and LAURIE, they are both overdressed for the occasion. JACK hangs all their outer garments on the coat rack. KAREN is hesitant to relinquish her purse, but finally sets it tentatively on the back corner of the buffet.

JACK: *(Grins and sniffs)* **MMmm! Something sure smells good in here!**

BRIAN: **Julia's cooking up a storm. Says she's making**

all our favorites.

LAURIE: *(Nodding)* **Yes, she says she wants our Christmas Eve dinner to be just like Mother used to make.**

JACK: *(Grins)* **Oh boy! I sure hope that means we're having Chocolate Surprise Pie for dessert!**

LAURIE: *(Rhetorically)* **That's right—I remember. You've always had a thing for Mom's chocolate surprise pie, haven't you?**

KAREN takes the gift from the table and moves to put the present under the tree.

KAREN: *(To no one in particular)* **My... what a... uh... beautiful tree! It's so... so... quaint.**

JACK: *(Under his breath)* **Not everyone insists on designer ornaments for their Christmas trees, Karen.**

KAREN: *(Tersely)* **I can see that...**

BRIAN stands and approaches JACK, shifting his glass to the left hand so he can shake hands.

BRIAN: **So, Jack!** *(Shakes hands, then puts the hand on Jack's shoulder, possibly for balance)* **So how've you been?**

JACK: *(Raises eyebrows)* **You mean since you missed our mother's funeral, or back before that?**

BRIAN: **Yeah, well, sorry I couldn't make it. Had to work, you know.**

KAREN: *(Cooly)* **So we heard.**

BRIAN: *(Ignoring her)* **So— how about I fix you two a drink?**

KAREN: *(Speaking right up)* **Thank you. I'll take a Perrier.**

BRIAN: **A what?**

LAURIE: *(Rolls eyes, then says pointedly)* **Karen wants a glass of water, dear.**

BRIAN: **Oh, well, why didn't she say so?** *(He crosses to the makeshift bar)* **And for you, Jack?**

JACK: **Nothing fancy. Whatever you're drinking is fine with me.**

BRIAN: *(Trying to make a joke)* **Well, you can't have what I'm drinking, cause *I'M* drinking it, but I'll be happy to fix you one just like it.** *(Big, silly grin, looks around waiting for response)*

When no one seems to get his joke, BRIAN shrugs and goes to buffet to get busy with the decanters. His back to the group. LAURIE goes to him and quietly whispers something in his ear.

KAREN: *(Looking aimlessly around)* **It was very nice of Julia to invite us all over for Christmas Eve, wasn't it?**

LAURIE: *(Returning to sit on couch)* **I guess.**

KAREN: *(Still standing)* **I mean it's nice that all you siblings are able to get together at the holidays like this.**

BRIAN: *(Hands drinks to Jack and Karen as he speaks)* **That's what Julia said your mother wanted—for us all to be together tonight. She said it was her dying wish.** *(Sits next to Laurie on couch)*

KAREN: *(Has not yet sipped drink. Now speaks all in a rush)* **Well, it's a good thing she died *this* year, cause next year at this time Jack and I will be in Aruba. We'll be gone for the entire month, and we aren't coming back for any family gatherings whatsoever, no matter what.**

Silence as they all turn to look at her, but she is totally oblivious, fidgeting with her cuffs, or collar, or arranging her bracelets or something.

JACK: *(Finally)* **Yeah... well... technically speaking, not all of us siblings are here tonight...**

Quiet for a beat as JACK and KAREN sit down at chairs bracketing fireplace. JULIA bustles in from kitchen.

JULIA: **Welcome! Welcome to my home! So glad you could make it.** *(Jack stands and she gives him a big hug and an air kiss on each cheek)*

KAREN: *(Clears throat)* **And I'm here, too.**

LAURIE: *(Under her breath to Brian)* **Oh, goody, now the party can start.**

JULIA: **Please sit down, everyone!** *(Goes to buffet and pours herself a drink)* **So… what did I miss?**

BRIAN: **Jack was just saying how not all of you siblings will be here tonight.**

JULIA: *(Softly)* **Oh… you mean Wesley.**

BRIAN: *(Confused, looks around)* **How many other siblings you guys got?**

LAURIE: *(Spits it out)* **Only one who now refuses to celebrate the holidays because that cult he joined forbids it.**

JACK: *(Sighs)* **I really thought he might make an exception this year.**

KAREN: *(Pragmatically)* **Well, that's one less gift to worry about.**

JACK: **Karen!**

KAREN: **Just sayin'...** *(Takes a sip of her water and makes a face)* **Hey! This isn't Perrier!**

BRIAN: *(To Laurie)* **You said she wouldn't notice.**

LAURIE: *(Shrugs)* **So I was wrong.**

JULIA: *(Sighs)* **Mom asked me to be sure to set six place settings** *(Looks toward table and shrugs)* **so I did as she requested.**

JACK: *(Soft smile)* **Maybe the sixth plate is for her.**

BRIAN: *(Like the theme from Twilight Zone)* **Do-do-do-do... Do-do-do-do... Do-do-do-do...**

Then all are quiet for a moment, reflecting, looking in their glasses, or at the tree, but not at each other.

KAREN: *(Breaking the silence)* **Is that dining table a Chippendale's?** *(She looks around expectantly)*

JULIA: **A what?**

KAREN: **A Chippendales! Jack got me a beautiful Chippendale's table for our very first anniversary.**

LAURIE: *(Eyebrows up in surprise, aside to Brian)*

Those Chippendales guys build furniture? I thought they were all just strip-tease dancers...

BRIAN: *(Aside to Laurie)* **Beats me. I thought 'Chip and Dale' were cartoon chipmunks.** *(He shrugs, palms up, with a "don't ask me" look on his face)*

KAREN opens her mouth to speak, but JACK quickly interrupts.

JACK: **Hey! I just thought of something!** *(He looks at JULIA)* **Do you have Mom's photo album?**

JULIA: **Which one?**

KAREN: *(Innocently)* **There's more than one?**

BRIAN: *(Laughing)* **There must be a half-dozen *boxes* of them!**

LAURIE: *(Sighs)* **Mother and her incessant picture taking.**

BRIAN: *(Laughs)* **I don't think she even set her camera down to eat when her grandkids were around.** *(Shakes head)* **Always snapping another damn photo.**

LAURIE: *(Nods)* **I'm just glad we didn't end up storing all those albums at our house.**

JACK: *(To Julia)* **The big red one. The very first one**

she put together—It's got all four of us in it when
we were just kids.

JULIA smiles and nods, and goes to the beverage buffet.
She brings forth a big red album from under the table or in
a drawer.

JULIA: **You mean this one?** *(She hands it to him)*

JACK: **Anyone want to take a little walk down**
Nostalgia Lane with me while we wait on dinner?

KAREN: *(Sighs)* **If this is going to get all mushy and**
melancholy, I'm going to need something
stronger than tap water.

KAREN goes to buffet to fix a drink while JACK pulls a
dining chair out to mid-stage and sits down. JULIA and
LAURIE pull chairs up, or stand behind him as he opens
the album. BRIAN joins KAREN at the buffet.

BRIAN: *(To Karen)* **If you're looking for melancholy,**
stand next to Julia. She's the emotional child.
(Beat) **At least that's what her mother always**
called her.

JULIA: *(Annoyed)* **At least I'm not a** *cold fish* **like**
some **people I could name—**

JACK: *(Quickly interrupting)* **And speaking of fish…**
(Points to picture in album) **Remember when we**
used to go camping and fishing over at Evergreen

Reservoir?

LAURIE: *(Squinting and leaning closer)* **Oh! There's the old Chrysler station wagon and the trailer with the monster overhang.**

JULIA: *(Laughing)* **Ah, yes, the trailer that slept six.**

JACK: **But only if you could sleep standing up!**

LAURIE, JULIA and JACK chuckle companionably. KAREN takes her drink and sits on the couch pretending to be totally disinterested, picking at her nails, occasionally sighing, and sipping her drink. BRIAN is still at the buffet.

BRIAN: *(Over his shoulder)* **How'd you guys go fishing at the reservoir without a boat?**

LAURIE: **Oh, we had a boat, all right. A 14-foot pram we carried on top of the car.**

BRIAN: *(Laughs)* **You guys must have looked like the Beverly Hillbillies traveling around like that.**

JULIA: *(Wistfully)* **I took a more romantic view of our weekend nomadic travels.** *(Sighs, smiles, voice becomes dramatic)* **I always thought we resembled the literary Joad family in Steinbeck's 'The Grapes of Wrath,' with all our belongings piled high in the car, along with many of our hopes and dreams—**

BRIAN: **The Joads? Never heard of them!** *(Looks around)* **They live around here?** *(He plops down beside KAREN, places his drink on the table and takes a handful of nuts)*

JULIA: *(Raises eyebrows, voice returns to normal, almost snide)* **Ok, then let's just say we were the Beverly Hillbillies without the money.** *(She takes a coaster from the beverage buffet and slaps it down under Brian's drink)*

JACK: *(Nodding)* **Mom used to cook the fish right there in the trailer almost as fast as we could catch them.**

LAURIE: *(Grins)* **Living off the lake, she called it.**

JACK: **No catch and release program for us; it was 'catch and eat'—or maybe it was 'if you don't catch, you don't eat.'** *(Laughs)*

KAREN: *(Mock Shudder)* **Sounds horribly uncivilized.**

BRIAN: **I dunno. Sounds like a good time to me.**

BRIAN pantomimes casting a fishing line with a "zzzing" sound and then reels it in, rocking back on the couch like he's really working at it.

LAURIE: **Careful dear, you'll hurt yourself.**

JULIA: *(Laughing)* **These were lake crappie and perch,**

Brian. Not all that hard to reel in. *(She sheepishly retrieves the apron from behind couch)* **Excuse me a minute while I check on dinner.** *(Exit)*

LAURIE reaches over into JACK'S lap and turns the album page.

JACK: *(Quickly starts to turn a second page)* **Oh, I think we can skip right by a few of these pages.**

LAURIE: **Oh no you don't!** *(Pause)* **Hey, Karen, ever see a picture of Jack in his fluorescent orange little Buster Barnett shirt?**

KAREN: *(Turning up her nose and remains seated)* **No, I never have, and quite frankly, I'd prefer it if I never do. Orange isn't his color.**

BRIAN: **A Buster Barnett shirt?**

JACK: *(Shrugs)* **That's just what Mom called them. They were short-sleeved, round-collared, three-button shirts.**

LAURIE: **And Mom put both her boys in those gawdawful orange shirts so she could spot them easily in the crowds at Disneyland.**

BRIAN: *(To Jack)* **Did you wear the mouse ears, too?**

JACK: **Don't remind me!**

BRIAN: *(Getting just slightly tipsy, singing)* **M-I-C, See you real soon! K-E-Y, Why? Because we like you!**

JACK and LAURIE: *(Good-naturedly join BRIAN singing)* **M-O-U-S-E.**

KAREN rolls eyes, sighs, shakes head, and does not join in the singing.

JULIA: *(Returns from kitchen wearing the holiday apron, wiping hands on dishtowel)* **You guys must be getting to the Disneyland pages.**

JACK: **Wrong! We've just *FINISHED* with the Disneyland pages.** *(Dramatically turns page)*

JULIA: **But you and Wesley were so adorable in your fluorescent shirts and Mousketeer ears!**

JACK: *(Scowls at her, then looks down at book)* **Oh look! Here's a *much* better photograph of me in my *manly* Little League uniform.**

BRIAN: *(Sitting up, interested)* **Oh yeah? What position did you play?**

KAREN gets up and goes to the buffet again, refilling her glass. She stands back by the dining room table, arms crossed between sips.

JACK: **First base.**

BRIAN: **An infield position!** *(Clasps hands)* **I knew it!** *(Nods, pause)* **Did Wesley play too?**

JACK: **Wesley pitched.**

LAURIE: *(Laughing)* **I remember Mother sitting in the stands with her hands over her eyes every time Wesley took the mound.**

JULIA: **Mother always swore it was Wesley's pitching that gave her her first ulcer.**

JACK: *(Knowlingly)* **Well, she may have said that, but I think it probably had more to do with the hotdogs she ate at our games.**

KAREN: *(Horrified)* **She actually *ATE* those disgusting things?**

BRIAN: *(Standing, but tipsy)* **Bases loaded, bottom of the ninth with two out. Wesley winds up and delivers the first pitch.** *(He mimes swinging the bat)* **Schwing… and a miss! Strike one!**

LAURIE: *(Goes to him)* **Hey there, Baby Ruth Bar, I think maybe you better have a seat.** *(To Julia)* **I think he needs to get some food into him pretty soon.** *(Seats Brian back on couch)*

BRIAN: **But… But… Hold on! I'm still at bat!**

KAREN: *(Shakes her head)* **Poor boy. I guess he just**

can't hold his liquor.

LAURIE: *(Between clenched teeth)* **Unlike some *other* people who aren't so affected because they drink all the time...**

JULIA: **Oh look!** *(Quickly pointing)* **There's a picture of Great Aunt Flora!**

JACK: **Did she ever *NOT* have gray hair?**

LAURIE: *(Goes back over to view the picture)* **Not in my lifetime, she didn't.**

JACK: **Truth be told, I don't think even Mom knew what color Aunt Flora's hair was when she was a young woman.**

LAURIE: **That's because Great Aunt Flora was never a young woman!**

All chuckle and nod knowingly.

KAREN: *(Rather snobbishly)* **Well, if you ask me, her hair always looked hideous—a rather steel gray-blue.**

LAURIE: **Well—duh! That's because she had the hairdresser put bluing on it!**

KAREN: *(Incredulously)* **You mean she had it done that way *on purpose?***

LAURIE: **Of course she did!**

KAREN: **Really?** *(Snorts or Hrrumphs in disbelief)* **I'd have sued somebody!**

BRIAN: *(Lifts his glass in salute)* **That's the problem with America today! Somebody's always suing somebody!**

KAREN: *(Sniffs, says indignantly)* **I'm just saying that I wouldn't be caught dead with hair the color of Aunt Flora's.**

LAURIE: *(Quietly aside)* **Now there's an interesting choice of words.**

JACK: *(Proudly)* **Karen, did I ever tell you that our family history, along Great Aunt Flora's side, dates straight back to the DAR?**

KAREN: *(Hopefully and brightly raises eyebrows)* **Discount And Retail?**

JULIA: *(Distainfully)* **That would be Daughters of the American Revolution, Karen.**

KAREN: **Is that supposed to *MEAN* something?**

LAURIE: *(Glaring)* **Apparently not to you.**

BRIAN: **Laurie's got her DAR Membership**

Certificate hanging in our den. It's one of her most prized possessions.

JULIA: *(Smiling, nods)* **Mine's hanging in my home office.**

KAREN: *(Haughtily)* **Why? What's the big deal?**

LAURIE: *(Draws out the first word)* **Because... Since we're not ever going to inherit anything of monetary value, our family history, dating clear back to the founding of this country, *IS* our inheritance.**

JULIA: **Hmmm... Speaking of inheritance...** *(Turning album page)* **I wonder...** *(Looks at Laurie and then Jack)* **Does anyone know whatever happened to the infamous walnut garland?**

LAURIE and JACK laugh with JULIA at the inside joke.

BRIAN: **Walnut garland?**

KAREN: *(Snottily)* **Don't demean yourself by asking, Brian. They obviously want to keep their private little secret all to themselves.**

JACK: **No, no, Karen, it's not like that at all. We'd be happy to share the story with you... wouldn't we Julia?**

JULIA: *(Shrugs)* **It all started way back when Aunt**

Flora was cleaning out the house she'd lived in for more than 75 years.

LAURIE: **Just before she went into Assisted Living.**

JULIA: *(Scowling at Laurie)* **You weren't even there.**

LAURIE: **Well, it's not like I haven't heard the story a few hundred thousand times.**

BRIAN: *(To Laurie)* **You have? How come you've never told *ME*?**

JULIA: **Like I was saying—Mother and Aunt Jo and I were there when Great Aunt Flora, who must have been 96 or 97 at the time, was cleaning out her house.**

BRIAN: *(To Laurie)* **How come you weren't there?**

JULIA: *(To Brian, with a smirk)* **Laurie was hiding in the outhouse so she wouldn't have to do the dishes after dinner.**

BRIAN: *(Looks from Julia to Laurie and back several times)* **What? Huh? I don't follow... Laurie was hiding *WHERE*?**

KAREN: *(Sighs, annoyed)* **It's another family insider joke, Brian. Let's just deal with one stupid story at a time.**

LAURIE: *(To Brian)* **I think I had to work that day.**

JACK: *(Hrrumphs)* **Yeah, right.**

JULIA: **At any rate, AF pulled a dark green string of yarn out of one of the boxes.** *(Holds hands out to illustrate)* **It wasn't more than a yard long.** *(Brian squints and estimates a yard with his own hands)*

LAURIE: *(Mimicking)* **...and then she ever-so-gently held the yarn out to Mother with her shaky, gnarled fingers...**

JACK: *(Laughing)* **Aunt Flora's hands always shook; you needed to be an expert in handwriting analysis to read any of her letters.**

KAREN: *(Motioning for quiet)* **Hush, Jack, let—one of them—continue.**

LAURIE: *(To Julia)* **You go ahead...** *(Smirks)* **You're the oldest...**

JULIA: *(Rolls eyes)* **Right. So anyway, this hank of yarn had maybe five or six gold-painted walnut shells glued along it.**

BRIAN: *(Puzzled, to Laurie)* **How'd she do that?**

LAURIE: *(Sighs, but speaks patiently, as if to a child)* **You crack the nuts very carefully, see** *(pantomiming)* **take the edible meats out, and**

then glue the empty shells back onto the yarn *(mimes again)* **about three or four inches apart.**

KAREN: **Are we ever going to get to the point, here, or am I going to need another drink before I hear the end of this story?** *(She goes to the buffet again and pours)*

LAURIE: *(Aside)* **Like she "needs" another drink?**

JULIA: *(Goes to sit near the fireplace)* **So, once again, as I was saying… Aunt Flora hands this ugly old piece of junk to Mother, and Mother takes it with two fingers like it's contaminated or something, and she just stares at it, distastefully.**

LAURIE: *(Aside to Brian)* **Well, really, what was she supposed to say?**

JULIA: *(Shrugs)* **And then AF nods her shaky head up and down a few times for emphasis and says,** *(Speaks in shaky voice)* **"I'm sure one of you girls will want to keep this—It's an heirloom, you know."**

KAREN: **An heirloom?!** *(Clasps hand to chest)* **Oh my GAWD!** *(Goes to couch and sits next to Brian)*

JULIA: *(Grins)* **I'll never forget the look on Mother's face. And Aunt Jo snorted so hard she had coffee spewing out of her nose!**

JACK: *(Laughing)* **Yeah, and then Mom tried to gracefully get out of taking it.**

LAURIE: *(To Julia)* **Hey, how come you don't chastise Jack for telling part of the story? He wasn't there either!**

JACK: **Yeah, but after all these years the story is kind of in the public domain, you know?** *(Beat)* **I don't think you really had to be there to know what happened next.**

KAREN: *(Annoyed)* **HELLO?? Your family folklore isn't exactly mainstream literature, you know. If it were, I'd just go on the Internet for the rest of the story and save you all the trouble.**

LAURIE: *(Enjoying this)* **Don't get your undies in a bunch Karen, we're almost there.**

BRIAN: **Yeah, so… did your mother end up taking the yarn or not?**

JULIA: **Well, for a couple minutes, Mother and Aunt Jo and I were all looking over the top of Aunt Flora's head making faces at each other.**

LAURIE: **And AF didn't have a clue as to what you were doing.**

JULIA: **No, not a clue. She was all misty-eyed, just gazing at that hank of yarn. I think she might** have been doing a little reminiscent time-traveling or something.

JACK: No telling what decade she was thinking about.

BRIAN: Wow! Now that you mention it, that string of walnut shells could have dated back before World War II, or maybe even World War I!

KAREN: *(Exasperated)* Oh, for crying out loud! I don't think they even *had* gold paint back then!

LAURIE: *(Patronizingly)* Ahhh… is someone getting cranky?

KAREN: *(Glares at Laurie)* The point is—speculating about what Aunt Flora was or wasn't thinking about when she looked at the walnut yarn is irrelevant.

JULIA: *(Checks her watch)* Maybe we should finish this story after dinner.

BRIAN and KAREN: *(Together shouting)* **NO!**

JACK: *(Shrugs)* I guess we better cut to the chase, Julia.

JULIA: Okay. *(Nods)* So then Mom says, "Oh, I think sister Pat should have it—after all, Pat's the oldest." *(All grin and nod)*

LAURIE: Then Aunt Jo pipes up and says, "And since

Pat's not here to accept it, I'll send it to her."

BRIAN: **Boy, I'll bet your Aunt Pat was sure surprised when a package arrived with that old piece of yarn in it.**

KAREN: **And… that's it? That's the end of the story?** *(Looks around confused)* **So what's the big deal?**

LAURIE: *(Distainfully to Karen)* **No, that's not the end of the story.**

BRIAN: **It's not?**

JACK: **Nope, it's not.** *(Pause)* **On every single Christmas after that, and on every birthday, one of those three sisters found that worn-out string of walnut garland tucked inside a gift package.**

JULIA: *(Grins)* **And then they started expanding the victim list!**

LAURIE: *(Nodding)* **I got it for my birthday one year, and sent it right off to Cousin Margie, cause her birthday was just a few weeks after mine.**

JACK: **And then Margie sent it to her sister inside a High School graduation gift.**

JULIA: **And I got it one year for Valentine's Day, disguised inside a heart-shaped box that used to contain chocolates.**

KAREN: *(Shaking her head, speaks to Jack)* **And were you boys included in this gift that keeps on giving?**

JACK: *(Laughing)* **No, Wesley and I had our own gift-giving tradition.**

KAREN: *(Fakes an exaggerated yawn)* **Do tell.**

JULIA: *(Smiles)* **I think you can relate this story without me, Jack.** *(Leaves again to the kitchen)*

JACK: **Well, one Christmas Wesley got a gas-powered model airplane. The kind that had dual lines attached so you could fly it around you in a circle.**

BRIAN: **Oh boy! I always wanted one of those!** *(Lifts both arms miming flying a dual-control model airplane, making noises as if it's coming closer and then fading out as it flies away)* **Nnnneeeoow!**

KAREN: *(Rolls her eyes at Brian, then speaks to Jack)* **And I suppose something happened to it?**

JACK: **Big time!** *(Laughs)* **The very first time we took it to the ball field to fly it, Wesley crashed it so hard it broke up into about a zillion pieces!**

LAURIE: *(Flings hands up and out)* **KA-BLUEY!**

BRIAN: *(Slumping back on couch)* **Oh, what a shame!**

LAURIE: **And then they scooped it all up into a cardboard carton, duct-taped it shut, and wrote "Airplane Parts" in felt pen all across the outside of the box.**

JACK: *(Shaking his head)* **We always swore we'd get around to rebuilding it someday, but we never found the time.**

KAREN: *(Puzzled)* **So what's that got to do with gift-giving?**

LAURIE: *(Laughs)* **Oh, that's the best part!**

JACK: **Just like with the walnut garland, we got very creative in passing that box back and forth between us.** *(Nods)* **First it was just for Christmases and Birthdays....**

LAURIE: **Yes, but then after Wesley starting refusing to celebrate those special events, the box started showing up at the oddest times and places.**

BRIAN: *(Sitting up)* **Oh yeah? Like where?**

JACK: **Well, one time my son Tyler spent the night at Wesley's house. And when he returned home,** *(Chuckles)* **that darn box was rolled up inside his sleeping bag.**

LAURIE: **And then when Jack went for a ride in Wes's**

new truck, Wesley later found the box was tucked behind the passenger seat.

JACK: **After that, Wesley left it inside the washing machine he was helping me install.**

KAREN: **Oh! Now I remember seeing that box!**

BRIAN: **And you guys just passed it back and forth between the two of you?**

JACK: **Yeah… It wasn't a family "heirloom" like Aunt Flora's walnut garland.** *(All laugh)*

JULIA returns to room, stands behind JACK and leans over him to turn a page in the album. All lapse into their own memories for a moment.

LAURIE: *(Quietly)* **Maybe this is why Mom insisted we all get together tonight—So we would remember the good times.**

JULIA: **I don't know…** *(Reflective)* **I've a feeling there's a lot more to it than that…** *(She rises and hands the photo album to Karen, turns to Jack)* **Jack— Would you mind giving me a hand with the ham? I need to get the side dishes into the oven.**

BRIAN: **Ham?** *(Looks around, confused)* **We're having ham? But… But…I had my taste buds all set for turkey.**

JULIA: **Gotcha!** *(Laughs)* **Yes, Brian, of course we're having turkey. It's Christmas! Mother would turn over in her grave if we ever messed with that tradition.**

KAREN: **Oooo, that's morbid.** *(She sets the album on the coffee table and goes to the bar, pouring several inches of amber liquid into a glass.)*

JACK: *(Stands to leave room)* **No, Karen, that's the truth! It has to be Turkey for Thanksgiving and Christmas, ham only on Easter.** *(Smiles)* **No discussion, no variations.** *(Laughs)* **Mother was very inflexible when it came to messing with family traditions!**

LAURIE: *(As Julia starts to leave)* **You don't need my help out in the kitchen, do you?**

JULIA: *(Looks back at Laurie, smiling and shaking her head)* **I'll take it that's rhetorical...** *(Exits)*

BRIAN: *(To Laurie)* **Why'd she say that?**

LAURIE: *(Trying to dismiss it)* **Just a little ancient family history, Brian, no biggie.**

JACK: *(Speaking back over his shoulder as he exits)* **Yeah, Brian, no biggie. Julia's holding a bit of a grudge from the time Laurie offered to help and set the kitchen on fire.**

BRIAN: *(Looks at Laurie)* **You really set Julia's kitchen on fire?**

KAREN: *(Taking a big swig from her glass)* **Ohhhh, I do-so want to hear more!**

LAURIE glares toward the empty kitchen doorway as the doorbell interrupts the conversation. They all turn toward the door in silence, but nobody makes a move. The bell sounds again.

JULIA: *(Calling out from offstage)* **Will somebody please get the door?**

Still, nobody moves toward the door.

BRIAN: *(Calling out toward kitchen)* **You think it's Wesley?**

JACK: *(Calling back)* **I sincerely doubt it.**

LAURIE: *(Eyebrows raised)* **Well, I'm pretty sure it's not Mother.**

KAREN: **Oh, for heaven's sake!** *(She dramatically marches to the door and yanks it open, the effect, no doubt of the alcohol)* **TA-DA!**

Rick Thomas enters the room, dressed in suit, tie, Santa Hat and red scarf. He is carrying two mid-sized wrapped and ribboned packages.

RICK: *(Loudly)* **Merry Christmas! HO! HO! HO! Merry Christmas!**

No one responds. They look at each other, puzzled, shrugging with a palms-up motion, shaking heads.

JACK: *(Re-entering room, he goes to Karen's side, but speaks to Rick))* **I'm sorry, but—do we know you?**

RICK: *(Looks around and quickly grasps the situation)* **Oh, no, I'm the one who's sorry! Forgive me! My name's Rick Thomas.**

KAREN: **And that's supposed to mean something?**

RICK: **I'm your mother's attorney.**

KAREN: *(Peering at him)* **Oh, no you're not!** *(Slurring a little)* **I'll have you know my husband's mother is dead! Dead as a doornail!**

RICK: *(Quickly, flustered)* **Oh, no, of course not. I mean yes, I know she is— Oh, dear. Please, let me start over!** *(Takes a deep breath)* **Alright now. My name is Rick Thomas, and I am your deceased mother's *FORMER* attorney.**

LAURIE: **I didn't know Mother had an attorney.** *(Others shake their heads and look baffled)*

RICK: **This is the Barnett residence, is it not?**

JACK: **Yes it is. My sister, Julia Barnett, lives here.**

RICK: **Then I assure you I am in the right place.**

KAREN: **The right place for what?**

RICK: *(Clears throat)* **I was entrusted by your mother, before her death of course, to bring these gifts here tonight.**

BRIAN: *(Half-rising, eyebrows up)* **Gifts? Gifts for who?**

KAREN: *(To Brian)* **That's WHOM.**

BRIAN: *(To Karen)* **Whom what?**

KAREN: **It's 'gifts for whom?'**

BRIAN: *(Losing patience, also slurring)* **I already asked that question already.**

RICK: *(Baffled by the exchange)* **I... uh... I believe the appropriate name tags are on them.**

BRIAN: *(Suspiciously)* **What's in them?**

RICK: **That, I'm afraid I cannot tell you, sir. The late Mrs. Barnett paid for my posthumous delivery services, but I was not privy to the specific contents of the parcels.**

KAREN: *(Slight slur)* **OOOooooo, he sounds just like a**

character in a spy novel! *(Calls out)* **Hey mister!** *(Peering at him)* **Are you a spy?**

JACK: **Karen, please, let's sit you down over here.** *(Leads her, unsteadily, to the couch and sits beside her)* **Here, have a mint.** *(He offers her the bowl from the coffee table)*

KAREN: **Oh, Vernell's buttermints! My favorite!** *(Takes several in each hand and shoves them all into her mouth.)*

RICK: **I assure you all, I am who I say I am.** *(Pause)* **My identification and business card are in my wallet, but, as you can see,** *(Shrugs)* **my hands are quite full.**

JACK: *(Stands)* **Here, let me take those from you.** *(Takes packages and remains standing there, waiting)*

RICK retrieves wallet from back pocket and produces two pieces of identification. He tries to hand them to JACK, but it is awkward, as now JACK'S hands are full, so he just holds them up for JACK to read.

JACK: *(To others, nodding)* **Well, he's got all the right credentials.**

RICK returns cards to wallet and takes back the presents.

RICK: **Now, if I may, I'd like to put these gifts under**

the tree and be on my way. (*Crosses room and bends down to do just that*)

JULIA enters, stage left. She takes a good look at the man putting presents under her tree and her eyes widen. She smiles and finishes wiping her hands off on the dishtowel she carries.

JULIA: (*Extending her hand*) **Well, hello there!** (*Big smile, as she shakes his hand*) **I'm Julia Barnett; I live here.** (*Waves her hands in the general direction of the others*) **And these poor unmannered souls are my siblings and their spouses.**

RICK: (*Shaking her hand*) **A pleasure to meet you, Ms. Barnett.** (*They hold eye contact for a beat*)

JULIA: (*Gushing, almost fawning*) **Oh, pullleeeze, you must call me Julia!**

RICK: (*A big smile, still holding her hand*) **Then you must call me Rick.** (*Looks around*) **You must all call me Rick!** (*Beat, then softer*) **And it's *STILL* a pleasure to meet you, Julia.**

Julia coyly giggles.

LAURIE: (*To Brian*) **Just exactly what is it we're watching here?**

BRIAN: (*To Laurie*) **I dunno, but if it goes on any longer, I think maybe we should make some**

popcorn.

JACK: *(To Julia)* **Did you know Mother had an attorney?**

JULIA: **Yes, of course I did.** *(Smiles at Rick)* **You're the one who drew up Mother's will, correct?**

RICK: *(Nods)* **Correct.**

JULIA: *(Coquettishly)* **We really should have met before now.**

RICK: *(Sighs, looking only at her)* **I certainly agree with you.** *(Then recovers his professionalism)* **But with advent of email, personal communications have become, uh, rather impersonal, I'm afraid.**

JULIA: *(Sighs and speaks only to him)* **Yes, they most certainly have...**

KAREN: *(Slight slur)* **Hey! Is this guy staying for dinner, or what?**

JULIA: **Yes! Yes of course! Please, Rick, you must stay for dinner!**

LAURIE: *(Pointedly)* **Unless, of course, you have a *WIFE* waiting dinner for you at home.**

RICK: **Wife? Uh... No... No wife; no girlfriend.** *(Waves bare left ring finger)* **I'm completely single.**

BRIAN: *(Shrugs)* **Then you might as well join us. It's a big turkey...** *(Pause, turns to Julia)* **It *IS* a big turkey, isn't it, Julia?**

JULIA: **Twenty-two pounds!**

KAREN: *(Slurring)* **Then the more, the merrier, that's what I always say!**

RICK: *(Hesitant, looks around questioningly)* **Oh, I wouldn't think of imposing on you and your family on Christmas Eve.**

JACK: **Believe me, it's not an imposition. Not at all. And since you came all this way on Christmas Eve just to fulfill a promise to my mother, it's the least we can do.**

JULIA: *(Batting eyelashes)* **Please say you'll stay. There's already a place set for you at the table...**

RICK: **There is?** *(Looks first at the table, and then using his index finger, silently counts the people in the room)* **Well, so there is.** *(Pause)*

JULIA: *(Happily)* **Then it's all settled. Here— Let me take your hat and scarf.**

RICK: **Well... All right, then...** *(He hesitantly hands Santa hat and scarf to Julia, who hangs them on the overflowing coat rack as he continues)* **Then I'd love** to have dinner with you—and your family, of course— *(Smiles)* And I will—but on one condition...

BRIAN: *(To Laurie)* **The nerve of this guy... setting conditions on his unexpected dinner invitation!**

LAURIE: *(To Brian)* **Shhhhh... Let's hear him out.**

JACK: *(Smiles patiently)* **And what condition would that be, Mr. Thomas— uh, I mean, Rick?**

RICK: **Well...** *(He looks tentatively at their faces)* **if you all don't mind, I'd love to know what's in those two packages. I've been holding onto them for the past couple of months, and I'm really quite curious.**

KAREN: *(Slight slur)* **Yeah, let's see what old Mumsy left us!**

Jack goes over to the tree and picks up the first package.

JACK: *(Looks at tag)* **It's for you, Laurie.**

LAURIE: **Me?**

JACK: **That's what it says.** *(He takes the package to where she's sitting)*

LAURIE: *(Looking around)* **Shall I open it?**

KAREN: *(Light slur)* **You're really not the sharpest knife in the drawer, are you, Laurie?**

LAURIE: *(Scowls at Karen)* **I just want to be sure it's all right with everybody.**

JULIA: **It's fine. Really. Now just rip it open!**

JACK: **Yeah, rip it open, Sis! Mother's not here, so you don't have to worry about saving any of the wrapping paper!**

All chuckle and nod knowingly.

JULIA: *(Giggles in Rick's direction)* **Oooo! I can't stand the suspense!**

Laurie tears the wrapping off the package and drops it on the floor. She opens the box and lifts out several wads of tissue paper before holding up a yard length of green yarn with gold-painted walnut shells glued along it. There is stunned silence for a moment.

RICK: **I don't understand.** *(Looks around)* **I've had that box secure in my office safe since your mother gave it to me. I thought it contained something very valuable.**

JULIA: *(Softly)* **It does, Rick... It most certainly does...**

JACK: *(Puts his hand on Laurie's shoulder)* **Do you feel it, Sis?** *(Pause)* **It's like Mom's right here with us.**

LAURIE: *(Trying to lighten the mood)* **Yeah, well, now I'm the one who's stuck with the darn thing…** *(Looks at Julia, smiles fiendishly)* **But maybe not for long!**

All laugh, or smile, or just exhale, nodding. Until Brian suddenly holds up his hand and waves it about to get their attention.

BRIAN: **Wait a minute! There's another package.** *(He teeters to the tree and picks it up)* **It's for Jack.** *(Hands it to him)*

JACK: *(Sits down with the package on his lap, looks around, and smiles reflectively)* **I don't even have to open this one, do I?**

JACK lifts the package up and gives it a hard shake. The sound of broken metal and plastic airplane parts is heard loud and clear.

JULIA: *(Laughs, pats Jack on shoulder)* **Merry Christmas, Jack. Merry Christmas from Mom!**

LAURIE: *(Nods thoughtfully)* **Yes. Merry Christmas, to one and all.**

BRIAN: *(Eyebrows suddenly go up)* **Hey! That turkey sure smells good!** *(Rubs his hands briskly together once more in anticipation)* **Let's eat!**

All stand and murmur Merry Christmas, good to see you, glad you're here, as they move toward the dining room table patting backs or companionably putting an arm around each other as they go.

Lights dim. CURTAIN CALL.

JAN BONO

Acknowledgments

I'd like to thank my family and friends for providing much of the "grist for the mill" included in this book. They've been a never-ending supply of entertaining moments throughout the past five decades.

And then there's Rick—without whom this book truly could not have come together. I know lots of authors say such things, but in this case, it's absolutely spot-on! Thank you, Rick, for all your technical assistance and constant moral support throughout this entire process. You're amazing!

Abundant blessings,
Jan Bono
September, 2011

Information on performing these Christmas plays, and a list of my many other books and plays is available on my website. Check out my blog!

www.JanBonoBooks.com